Praise for *The FT Guide to* ▮

'Despite years of sales and training exper▮
Networking I found it really hard to do. C▮
a lot about networking; then I read this excellent, insightful ▮
only to find out so much more about business networking. It is written in
an easy to read, down to earth style that makes it simple to learn lessons
(and there are loads of them). Even if you are an experienced networker
(combining online and offline), I highly recommend you read this book.

'If you are new to networking, nervous about or not getting enough results
from your networking – you definitely need to buy this book.'

Jon Baker, business coach with *Venture-now*

'If you ever thought face-to-face or social networking was difficult or would
not work for you – think again! This book makes it easy and really shows
why networking online and offline should be your first choice in how to
do more business, more enjoyably than ever before. It should be your networking Bible!'

Bruce King, author of How to Double Your Sales

'If you want to achieve workplace success, and build a strong personal brand,
then business networking is critical. Take the first step to understanding
and implementing networking strategies by reading Heather's book!'

Dan Schawbel, author of Me 2,0 and founder of Millennial Branding, LLC

'The most relevant, current and comprehensive guide to business networking available.'

Mick Holloway, co-founder of NetLinked

'If business networking was an applied science, Heather Townsend's book
would be the curriculum, survival guide and roadmap to this often misunderstood aspect of life and business. Having studied and interviewed the UK's
and the world's top thought leaders on the subject, coupled with her own
practical experience, this book offers an objective overview, discussing business networking's global principles, which are clearly laid out and explained.

'Whether it be face-to-face, or making connections through Twitter, every
aspect of connecting with others is uncovered and explained. Readers can
hope to have a shifted perception about how they should view networking
but, most importantly, to learn how to stop wasting time and invest in
the actions which, further down the line, will lead to personal referrals or
valuable connections – the end goal. This guide should be read by entrepreneurs, job seekers, employees at all levels and, in my opinion, high-school
kids ready to take on the world. Nothing evangelical, easy-to-read, practical
and highly recommended.'

David Stoch, director, Meerkat PR

'There are few people as proficient as Heather in both face-to-face and online networking. Queen of Twitter and founder of the impressive Executive Village network, she shares her knowledge in a very practical way in this really valuable handbook. It will give you the confidence and tools you need to excel in both worlds, joining up your on- and offline activity for networking success. I'd recommend this book to anyone in business – whether you are looking to build a company or boost your professional career.'

Sonja Jefferson, director, Valuable Content

'Heather delivers the ultimate guide for the ultimate business tool of the 21st century. Business networking is, in the 2010s, what talent management was during the 2000s. It is the essence of sustainable competitive advantage for business. As "talent management" was deemed by some, to their detriment, to be a load of "mumbo jumbo" nonsense, the same can be said of attitudes to networking. Networking is one of those areas where you need to ask yourself "Can you afford not to?" rather than "Can I spare the time for this?"

'Heather's *Guide to Business Networking* covers all the "etiquette" that enables people to develop into effective networkers, whilst not being so prescriptive that it stifles individuality. The guide covers all the different "media" by which networking can take place. A guide for those new to networking, as well as those "older heads" that need to re-evaluate or refine their approach.

'A must read.'

Marc Lawn, founder of The Business GP

'More so now than ever it is crucial for all business professionals to actively develop and grow their networks daily. Through sharing stories of real life successes, Heather brings the art of joined-up networking to life.

'The many tips, activities and suggestions aid both novice and expert networkers alike to create a bespoke strategy for business networking; developing an individually tailored approach that uses a wide variety of traditional methods and modern media that is right for them.

'Acting on the tried and tested FITTER™ approach gives you both jam for today and more importantly helps you build a network that will provide jam for tomorrow.

'Since reading this book, I can genuinely say I have come away fired up to build on already strong networks to get them to deliver more results for me!'

Karen Spillane, learning and development professional

The Financial Times Guide to Business Networking

The Financial Times Guide to Business Networking

How to use the power of online and offline networking for business success

Second edition

Heather Townsend

Harlow, England • London • New York • Boston • San Francisco • Toronto • Sydney • Auckland • Singapore • Hong Kong
Tokyo • Seoul • Taipei • New Delhi • Cape Town • São Paulo • Mexico City • Madrid • Amsterdam • Munich • Paris • Milan

PEARSON EDUCATION LIMITED
Edinburgh Gate
Harlow CM20 2JE
United Kingdom
Tel: +44 (0)1279 623623
Web: www.pearson.com/uk

First published 2011 (print and electronic)
Second edition published 2014 (print and electronic)

© Heather Townsend 2011, 2014 (print and electronic)

The right of Heather Townsend to be identified as author of this work has been asserted by her in accordance with the Copyright, Designs and Patents Act 1988.

Pearson Education is not responsible for the content of third-party internet sites.

ISBN: 978-1-292-00395-5 (print)
       978-1-292-00521-8 (PDF)
       978-1-292-00520-1 (ePub)
       978-1-292-00519-5 (eText)

British Library Cataloguing-in-Publication Data
A catalogue record for the print edition is available from the British Library

Library of Congress Cataloging-in-Publication Data
Townsend, Heather.
  The financial times guide to business networking : how to use the power of online and offline networking for business success / Heather Townsend. -- Second edition.
    pages cm
  Includes bibliographical references and index.
  ISBN 978-1-292-00395-5 -- ISBN 978-1-292-00521-8 (PDF) -- ISBN 978-1-292-00520-1 (ePub)
  -- ISBN 978-1-292-00519-5 (eText)
  1. Business networks. I. Title.
  HD69.S8T69 2014
  650.1'3--dc23
                              2014016164

The screenshots in this book are reprinted by permission of Microsoft Corporation.

10 9 8 7 6 5 4 3 2 1
18 17 16 15 14

Cover image © Getty Images

Print edition typeset in 9/13pt ITC Stone Serif by 3
Print edition printed and bound in Great Britain by Ashford Colour Press, Gosport

NOTE THAT ANY PAGE CROSS REFERENCES REFER TO THE PRINT EDITION

Contents

Part 4   Putting your joined-up approach to networking into action

About the author

Heather Townsend helps professionals become the Go-To Expert. She is the co-author of *The Go-To Expert* and *How to Make Partner and Still Have a Life*, and a high-profile member of the professional services industry. Over the last decade, Heather has worked with over 300 partners, and coached, trained and mentored over 2,000 professionals at every level of the world's most ambitious professional practices.

Heather is a full member of the Professional Speaking Association. She speaks regularly at large conferences within the professional services sector. In 2011 and 2012 Heather judged the British Accountancy Awards. In 2013 Heather was voted by the ICAEW's *economia* magazine one of the top 50 influencers on social media for finance and business.

Heather is increasingly gaining a reputation as a fresh thinking, astute, practice management expert. She writes regularly for the trade press and often is quoted in the national press.

Acknowledgements

Writing this book in 2010 lead me on the most amazing and personally satisfying professional journey. Therefore, it has been a real privilege to be given the opportunity to write a second edition. Re-reading the original text has brought back good memories which has made writing it a real pleasure.

I'd like to thank several people – what author doesn't? Firstly, there is Jon – my business partner and rock. Without him the first edition, and many other things as well, would never have been finished. There is also my mastermind group who I have now met up with weekly for many years. The guidance I receive from Lee, Ian, Rob and Jonathan may at times be tough to hear, but it is always incredibly valuable.

My editor, Robert Watson, has now worked on all three of my books and is a lifelong friend. Who would have thought a relationship such as this could have started with just one tweet?

Then there are all the people who kindly gave up their time to be interviewed for this book, whose collective experiences and stories helped shape my own thinking and ideas: Ivan Misner, Guy Clapperton, Brad Burton, Andy Lopata, Dan Schawbel, Brian Inkster, Hamish Taylor, Mike Briercliffe, Anthony Lloyd, Gary Ives, Jon Shaw, Jonathan Senior, Neil Ryder, Bryony Thomas, Mariam Cook, Melissa Kidd, Karen Spillane, Gina Wadsworth, Eli Barbary, Maggie Langley, Autumn St John, Jeremy Marchant, Alicia Cowan, Wendy Johnson, Sharon Gaskin, Lisa Williams, Elaine Clark, Maxine Welford, Lisa Garwood, Babs Morse, Martin Bragg and Charlie Lawson.

And, finally, there are three people who are the reason I get up in the morning (often far earlier than I would like!). I just want them to be as proud of me as I am of them and to return my unconditional love.

Publisher's acknowledgements

We are grateful to the following for permission to reproduce copyright material:

Text
Article on page 219 from 'Networking becomes a dirty word', *Financial Times*, 02 February 2014 (Bearden, N.), © Neil Bearden; Article on page 221 from 'Putting a price on your contacts', *Financial Times*, 22 January 2014 (Palmer, M.), © The Financial Times Limited. All Rights Reserved; Article on page 224 from 'Naked bosses and other gym hazards', *Financial Times*, 26 January 2014 (Rigby, R.), © The Financial Times Limited. All Rights Reserved; Article on page 225 from 'If I was … wanting to switch careers', *Financial Times*, 12 February 2014 (Polhemus, R.B.), © Polhemus, R.B.; Article on page 227 from 'The importance of bridging the cultural divide', *Financial Times*, 08 December 2013 (Knight, R.), © The Financial Times Limited. All Rights Reserved; Article on page 228 from 'MBA gender gap: tips on networking', *Financial Times*, 19 November 2013 (Clarke, C.), © The Financial Times Limited. All Rights Reserved.

Figures
Figure 10.3 from A.N.G. Creative Design.

In some instances we have been unable to trace the owners of copyright material, and we would appreciate any information that would enable us to do so.

'We are living in a knowledge economy in which the first thing to recognise is no single person is smart enough by themselves to be genuinely successful.'

Hamish Taylor, Shinergise Partners Ltd, www.shinergise.com

Introduction

The phone rang late on a snowy Friday afternoon just before the start of the Christmas holidays. It was Lee Duncan, a member of my virtual mastermind group, with some work for me from one of his contacts, to run a social media workshop in January. Was this luck? Serendipity? Far from it. This phone call was proof that the best way to advance your career and business is via networking.

My interest in joined-up networking – the art of combining face-to-face networking with online networking – started when I found myself at the wrong end of a corporate downsizing. My in-house network suddenly vanished and I had to create a new network in a world of strangers. Early into my life as a business owner, I quickly found that the easy way to generate work for myself was via the people I knew. With a very young family, and client work that could take me away for days at a time, I turned to online networking to supplement my face-to-face networking efforts. It was this winning combination of face-to-face and online networking that enabled me to single-handedly build a business which, within two years, generated an annual income significantly greater than my previous salary. My network, and my continual focus on networking activities, is the reason why my business has skyrocketed and become one of the few start-up businesses that are still trading five years on. It's also the reason I was approached to write this book.

I am not an isolated example – for a professional, networking is the fastest and most effective way to build a business or career. Professionals report that 80 per cent of their business comes from people they know. They know that networking, done correctly, will increase your pool of contacts, build awareness of what you do, motivate those valuable referrals and identify career-enhancing job openings. If you network effectively, the relationships you create will generate a stream of opportunities from which you can choose. As you will discover in this book, many successful professionals generate all their business through networking activity alone.

In the past, networking was an activity conducted face-to-face: through formal and informal groups such as professional associations, networking clubs, breakfast meetings and events. These remain important today, but with the meteoric rise of online forums and social networking sites, networking on the web has now really come into its own. Sites such as LinkedIn, Facebook and Twitter enable busy professionals to manage networks of contacts many times larger than is possible face-to-face and to generate consistent opportunities without even leaving their desks. This book will show you how to build a successful joined-up networking strategy, which will allow you to pick the most effective mix of networking activities for you.

With the benefit of hindsight, when I wrote the first edition in 2010 online networking was still very much in its infancy. In the last four years, this has changed and any savvy networker needs to be using both online *and* offline networking. The internet has now set the expectation that we can find anything, anyone or any information online. Consequently, geographical barriers are tumbling down as people are now able and conditioned to find *the* expert they need via the internet. The *Financial Times* Effective Client-Adviser Relationships 2012 report found that 40 per cent of all professional service buyers had, in their top three buying criteria, a requirement to work with a sector specialist who had a deep understanding of their business and marketplace.

Trust, traditionally, has always been generated via a face-to-face relationship with people. Today, trust can also be built up by the presence you maintain online and the content you regularly share with others. As a result, the personal brand you build is more important than ever. Whilst you can still achieve many things by using only face-to-face methods, you will gain results much quicker if you embrace a mix of both online and offline networking.

In 2011, I was approached to help the largest face-to-face networking organisation in the UK, BNI, add social networking and social media into everything they did. As a result of their investment in social media, they have found that they, unlike most networking organisations, have maintained rather than suffered a reduction in membership levels. Charlie Lawson, UK national director for BNI, has found that his investment in social media, particularly Twitter, has helped him get much closer to his grassroots members.

During the past 10 years, I have trained and coached more than 3,000 professionals at every level of a business. As a result, I've observed first hand that networking is a core competency that any business professional must master, whether you are looking to move up the career ladder internally or set up and grow your own practice or business. There are thousands of books and training resources on how to use social media, face-to-face networking and referral generation. Even though this book is now in its second edition, I still believe that this is the only single resource for professionals on what is needed to excel in both arenas, i.e. how to join up your networking efforts, saving time and generating results more easily for greater business and career success.

Who is this book for?

This book is written for business owners, people with business development responsibilities, job seekers and professionals – lawyers, bankers, accountants, coaches, trainers, advisors and consultants: experts in their field with specialist skills, typically for hire. In today's business world, regardless of whether you should sell your time for money, your time really does equate to money. For this reason you have to constantly balance the day job, your own profile and visibility, and potentially marketing your services to get more clients. In this book you will find practical guidance to help you network efficiently so that you can maximise your productive time and deliver exceptional service and results. Networking is an immensely valuable but time-consuming tool. As Rob Brown, author of *How to Build Your Reputation*,[1] said: 'You don't get paid for networking, you get paid on the results of your networking.' Joining up and integrating your online and offline activities will get you better results for far less effort.

Most professionals know that effective networking is vital if they want to be successful in what they do. Some may have years of experience of networking in person but be daunted by the world of online networking. Others are a whiz at social networking on the web but enter any face-to-face networking event with extreme trepidation. Many professionals don't network well at all. This is dangerous: get it wrong and at best you'll lose out on opportunities; at worst you can severely damage your professional credibility.

This book teaches you the skills you need to avoid the pitfalls and excel at networking both online and face-to-face. It will help you feel equally comfortable when building business relationships face-to-face or via social

---

[1] Brown, R., *How to Build Your Reputation: The secrets of becoming the 'go to' professional in a crowded marketplace*, Ecademy Press, 2007.

networking, and help you use your time efficiently and get best results by combining the two.

For those who network well, the rewards are huge: get your personal contacts to do your marketing for you and you won't need to worry about where the next client or job is coming from – you can pick and choose your ideal assignments and focus on delivering the best service to your clients.

What has been updated in the second edition?

The pace of technological advancement is relentless. As a consequence parts of this book, particularly the chapter on online networking options, has been comprehensively updated to reflect the changes in online networking.

From my workshops with professionals on networking, I know that regardless of how experienced you are, going into a room full of strangers to 'network' is almost universally disliked. I have included more information in this chapter to help anyone feel more confident when working the room.

I have added a new chapter focused on helping you ask for introductions and referrals from your network. As I found, to my cost, much of what has been written on 'how to ask for referrals' doesn't work outside of a formal networking group. As many of my clients have moaned to me that their team just 'wouldn't proactively ask for referral', this chapter will be a welcome addition to them and many others!

Many of my readership from the first edition of this book have commented on how much they have enjoyed and been inspired by the case studies in the book. As a result of this feedback, I've included more real-life case studies of how people have used networking (and tools from the first edition of this book) to generate career and business success, such as gaining a new job, successfully starting a new business and moving seamlessly from being employed to freelancing.

How to use this book

This book is written so you can either read from cover to cover or dip in and out.

At the end of each chapter are:

■ exercises for you to do to put into practice what you have just learned

■ links and references to further resources.

The book is split into four discrete parts.

Part 1 The joined-up approach to business networking

Part 1 concentrates on the thinking behind a successful approach to business networking. In this section we explore:

■ what networking is and isn't

■ the four ingredients needed for a successful joined-up networking strategy

■ the behaviours and attitudes of great networkers.

Part 2 Online and face-to-face networking options explored

Part 2 identifies all the different types of networking available today and how to maximise your effectiveness with each type. In this part you will discover:

■ where and when you should network online or in person

■ how to make best use of your time when networking, regardless of where you are networking

■ the pros and cons of each different type of networking

■ how to use your blog to increase the impact of your networking.

Part 3 Essential networking skills for the joined-up networker

Part 3 helps you acquire the necessary skills to excel as a networker. You will find out how to:

■ make a great first impression with everyone you meet

■ effectively work a room

■ create a connection and start a positive relationship with everyone you meet – regardless of where you meet them or their cultural background

■ ask for referrals and introductions

■ turn your network into your own online community

■ use a checklist to help you network efficiently.

Part 4 Putting your joined-up approach to networking into action

Part 4 brings together everything you have learned and prompts you to devise your own successful joined-up networking strategy and plan. You will learn how to:

- set your own networking goals to generate the business and career success you need
- use your network to find a new job
- generate referrals via your network
- become more confident as a networker
- measure the progress you are making with your networking activities
- decide who you need to recruit into your network
- make the most of the time and resources you have available to network.

At the end of the book you will find a section on additional resources to help you continue your networking journey, such as:

- suggested books and blogs on different aspects of networking
- contact details for networking groups
- instructions to download worksheets and templates referenced in this book.

And finally

Come and have a chat with me on Twitter, @heathertowns, connect with me on LinkedIn, www.linkedin.com/in/heathertownsend, look for me on Google+, or drop me a line at heather@heathertownsend.co.uk. I'd love to hear your networking success stories and will publish the best on www.joinedupnetworking.com – my blog on networking.

part

1

The joined-up approach to business networking

If I say networking to you, what do you think about? I would hazard a guess that most of you will have thought about a group of strangers in a room talking to each other.

Is this what we really mean by business or professional networking?

Part 1 of this book will first dispel the commonly held view that networking is all about talking to strangers at an event, and define for you what networking is and isn't. It will then dig deeper into the four ingredients needed for your joined-up networking to be successful. Then, finally, we look at the behaviours and attitudes that define great networkers.

1

Why network?

What topics are covered in this chapter?

- How networking can positively benefit your business and career
- Why networking is misunderstood or avoided
- What networking is and what it is not
- Why invest time in building your network now, and how much time it will take
- The powerful benefits of including online and face-to-face networking in your networking strategy
- How the skills and tools for both types of networking are complementary
- When to use online or face-to-face networking

By the end of this first chapter you'll understand why networking is such a useful tool for people today and the opportunity it presents if you get it right. You'll learn why many people get it wrong or avoid it. We'll introduce you to face-to-face and online networking and explain why a networking strategy that combines the two will get you the best results.

'You are now competing with everyone on a global scale. There is no job security at all, and now it is all about being found instead of submitting your resume. Networking is the way to be found, and how the smart people get jobs and opportunities now. That is the big difference from even five years ago.'

Dan Schawbel, author of Me 2.0: Build a powerful brand to achieve career success[1]

---

[1] Schawbel, D., *Me 2.0: Build a powerful brand to achieve career success*, Kaplan Trade, 2010.

Whether you are advancing your career or developing your own business, networking is *the* most effective way to build awareness, get found and generate opportunities. Go and sit in a café near your work at lunchtime and tune in to the chatter around you – chances are you'll overhear a conversation that goes something like this:

'You are thinking of redoing your website/contacting a recruitment consultant/changing accountants? The person you should be talking to is X.'

Through effective networking activity *you* can become the known and recommended expert in your field. And the power of recommendation is extremely strong. Most high-value purchases, such as hiring a new employee or engaging a new supplier, involve an element of risk. It's this risk that is why someone will always place more faith and trust in a recommendation rather than someone unknown to them or their network.

Get your networking right and others will do the job of selling for you, spreading the word about your services, products or skills – your own sales force happy to spot opportunities on your behalf, and for free!

'Our networking activities led to our profit and turnover doubling every year for the last four years, even through the credit crunch and recession.'
Gina Wadsworth, partner in Contact Consultants and director of BNI, the world's largest networking organisation[2]

Effective networking will build your profile, generate genuine opportunities for you – new career opportunities, new partners, new clients. It will extend the strength of the community around you and help you find the answers and tools you need to solve your business problems.

You could have the best product or service out there, or be the most amazing employee to hire but, if no one knows about it or you, how are you going to be found? That's why it is so important for any professional to develop and maintain a strong network of people who can help spread the word about your products, services or skills.

❝Networking has always been a highly effective tool❞

Networking has always been a highly effective tool. As long as commerce has existed, traders have banded together for the common protection against enemies, to govern the conduct of trade and help each other out. Chambers of commerce, which have traditionally provided a hub for networking activities, have been in existence since the

1700s. But in today's global, knowledge-based economy, networking has really come to the fore. We have far greater choice and access to people than ever before, but less time or inclination to spend on finding the right person for the job. This is why people are now using their networks more and more – to help them rapidly get to the best solution at the first time of asking. With the rise of online networking via social media you can now build a far larger and more engaged network more easily and more quickly than ever before.

Lack of investment in building a strong network will leave you exposed when you need to find new opportunities – be they a new job or new clients. The most effective way to find a new job or new business is via your network. However, a strong network takes time to build and nurture, and will start to bear fruit only once this is done.

case study

Jon Shaw, an IT project manager, needed a new job fast. His soon-to-be ex-employers decided to shut his office two years earlier than originally planned, in the process making him and many other employees redundant. Jon used LinkedIn to communicate to his network that he was in the market for a new job. One month later, after many phone calls and meetings with his network, a friend recommended Jon for a six-month contract position, which hadn't yet been formally advertised. Jon was hired subsequently for the contract position and, after three months in the role, was offered the job on a permanent basis.

case study

Little did Jeremy Marchant, co-owner at Emotional Intelligence at Work, realise how important his relationship with Dave, a Business Link skills advisor, would actually turn out to be. As a result of the relationship, which Jeremy and Dave built up over three lunches, Jeremy has received a steady stream of work from Dave's referrals and recommendations. One of these pieces of work ended up being a lucrative 16-month stress management programme within a local hospital.

Why networking is misunderstood or avoided

Does this sound familiar? Work is a little thin on the ground for your company, so the edict comes down from on high: *'Everyone needs to get out networking to drum up business.'* Or your manager is telling you: *'You need to get out there and network to improve your profile.'* You've received no training on how to network and suddenly you are required to be out there 'networking'. Whatever that actually means...

Sadly, this is an all-too-common occurrence in business. Is it any wonder that people often hate networking and will go to great lengths to avoid actually having to network, particularly when many organisations expect their staff to network in their own time rather than on company time?

Networking is probably one of the most misunderstood skills that today's workforce need for career and business success. It is not:

■ the start of the sales process

■ a cosy chat

■ solely about meeting new people or 'working a room'.

It is these misunderstandings that mean many people can 'blunder' into networking, whether face-to-face or online and, due to a lack of skill, become ineffective networkers. After a while, most people, when hitting their head against a brick wall, stop. It's the same with networking – if you don't get any results in the short or medium term, quickly you will become disheartened with networking and give up.

This lack of networking ability causes many people to stop networking. How much easier is it to meet new people if you know how to start a conversation or relate to anyone you meet? How less scary is a room full of people talking if you know how to break into and out of groups? How much nicer is everyone you meet when you are not trying to sell them something?

'To stand up for the first time in a networking meeting and talk about my business for 60 seconds was the most terrifying thing of my entire life.'
Gina Wadsworth, partner at Contact Consultants and BNI director

Many businesses, often through ignorance or fear, still routinely block their employees' access to social networking sites such as Facebook, LinkedIn and Twitter. These are all fantastic online networking tools, which, as I've found for my business and career, are essential tools for today's savvy networkers. Even amongst those people who can access online networking sites at work, many don't know how or where to start with online networking or struggle to gain sufficient momentum to generate results from their time and effort. Consequently, many networkers' efforts at online networking fizzle out after a couple of weeks. For example, according to an AYTM Market research study conducted in 2012, 42 per cent of Twitter users rarely tweet.[3]

ɢɢWhat incentive do you have to network?ɟɟ Successful networkers invest time and energy growing and maintaining their network. For example, Karen Spillane, a training professional, spends 30 minutes every day keeping in touch with her network. Many people, when faced with a high workload and/or family responsibilities, see networking as a luxury rather than a necessity. If you are being measured only on what you achieve in your day job, what incentive do you have to network?

I worked part time for a couple of years after my children were born. I thought my job was pretty secure, I didn't have any business development responsibility, and I was enjoying what I was doing. Why did I need to network? More importantly, between work and family, when did I have time to network? Whilst you may not be a busy working parent, it is a common phenomenon – many people don't see a reason to network. They have access to all the answers they need within their current setup, they are not responsible for business development, and they are happy in the job they are in. So, why network? When the recession hit in the UK, many people, myself included, realised that their job wasn't all that secure, and the lack of investment in their network had left them very exposed.

What networking is and what it is not

At its very simplest, networking is about meeting people and interacting with them. Effective business networking is the process of building up mutually beneficial relationships for your career or business.

Professionals fundamentally network for four reasons:

1 To improve their profile, i.e. being 'found'.
2 To generate opportunities, such as a new job or new clients.
3 To extend and strengthen the community around them.
4 To find answers and 'tools'.

---

[3] http://aytm.com

When you talk about networking, many people connect networking merely with formal networking clubs and associations such as BNI, the world's largest business networking organisation. However, without realising it, most of us are networking consistently throughout our waking hours. You may not badge all these activities as networking, but they are all ways in which we network:

■ Phoning your mother or a friend for your regular catch-up.

■ Writing and posting up a new blog post.

■ Introducing yourself to a new member of your club or society.

■ Exchanging some pleasantries on a phone call before getting down to business.

■ Logging into your Facebook account and reading your friend's status updates.

■ Attending a friend's wedding.

■ Inviting your work colleagues over for a meal.

■ Answering a question posted on an online forum.

■ Regularly attending a business networking club.

■ Updating your Twitter account with what you have had for lunch.

■ Telling your partner about what happened to you at work today.

■ Talking to the person next to you in the queue for coffee at a conference.

■ Going for drinks after work with your team.

What networking is not is *pitching*. Too often people see networking as the start of the sales process, and it is the most common mistake people make when networking. Effective networking is not about selling or asking for a new job, it is about developing strong relationships in which work and opportunities will come via, not from! If you are mistakenly selling whilst out networking, you will be unpopular and damage your credibility.

'People at networking events often don't want to meet lawyers and accountants and network with them, because they tend to get pitched to. This is the reason many professionals sometimes find networking events inhospitable.'

*Andy Lopata, co-author of ...*And Death Came Third![4]

---

[4] Lopata, A., and Roper, P., ...*And Death Came Third! The definitive guide to networking and speaking in public*, Ecademy Press, 2nd revised edn, 2011.

Why invest time in building your network right now

Many people start to network proactively when they want something, for example a new job or new clients. This is too late. Core to any networker's continual success are strong relationships built on a foundation of trust. These relationships and trust don't appear magically on a first or second meeting; they take time to establish. This means that it is best to build and invest time in your network at least six months before you need to call upon it.

Smart people are using networking in order to be found and get the best pieces of business and assignments. What are you personally missing out on by not proactively networking?

The time investment needed for networking

'The main problem we all have in business is a lack of time. Time is our most valuable resource. That's why networking is key to success for today's professionals. Successful networkers invest time nurturing and building their network, so their network does most of the work of generating leads, referrals and new business for them.'

Gina Wadsworth, partner at Contact Consultants and BNI director

Networking takes time. You and I both know that time equals money in your world. Effective networking is the most efficient way to generate the results you require for your business and career success. Throughout this book, you will read about how others network effectively, and the resultant time they invest in their networking activities. I am not suggesting, as a result of reading this book, you copy their example; you need to find the right level of networking for you personally. Let me give you an example. Many people want to know how I manage to generate 90+ per cent of my business via my networking activity, basically so that they can replicate my success! When they hear about the time investment taken to do that, often they decide they can't, in fact, afford to spend the time. At the end of the day, it's all about personal choice. You have a choice about how much time you will spend networking, by what means you will network, and how much success you will generate for yourself when networking.

As you read through this book, I encourage you to think of small things that you could add easily into your day that will make a positive difference to your career or business.

Why include both online and face-to-face networking in your networking strategy

'It's now not about face-to-face networking *or* online networking, it is about *and*.'

Ivan Misner, founder of BNI

In the last 10 years the tools available to networkers have increased drastically with the arrival of online networking. In the past, networking was an activity conducted face-to-face through formal and informal groups such as professional associations, networking clubs, breakfast meetings and events. Your little black book of contacts probably still was a black book or Rolodex!

These face-to-face networking events remain important today, but with the meteoric rise of sites such as LinkedIn, Twitter and Facebook (to name a few), networking on the web now has come into its own. As global virtual teams become increasingly prevalent, a successful professional has to transcend organisational, cultural, functional and geographical boundaries... but still we can be in only one physical place at any one time!

Sites and software such as LinkedIn and Twitter enable busy professionals to manage large networks of contacts across cultural, functional and geographical boundaries – many times larger than is possible face-to-face – and to generate consistent opportunities for those people prepared to invest time in them.

If you haven't yet added online networking into your networking strategy, one of your competitors definitely has, and they will be generating opportunities that previously may have come your way. By using online networking and face-to-face networking, rather than just face-to-face networking alone, your competitors will be getting more quickly to the people who can help them achieve their goals. For example, Cathy Richardson, a UK-based headhunter who specialises in the automotive industry, uses her LinkedIn network to identify and find potential candidates. When she is looking for suitable candidates, she is more likely to contact those with a complete and active LinkedIn profile. Can you or your business afford not to combine online networking with face-to-face networking?

How skills and tools for both types of networking are complementary

'In the new world of social networking, the same rules for face-to-face networking still apply.'

Guy Clapperton, journalist and writer of This is Social Media: Tweet, blog, link and post your way to business success[5]

In reality most face-to-face networking is about people standing around and talking to each other. Online networking is no different. The location may change to an internet forum or social networking site, but it is still people standing around and talking to each other. It's how well you do this 'standing around and talking', whether face-to-face or online, that will determine your success as a networker.

❝Treat people in the online world with courtesy and respect❞

I have found that the skills needed to succeed in online networking are just the same as face-to-face networking – it is still about how you meet, engage and maintain your relationships with people. Treat people in the online world with courtesy and respect, and trust will build within your online relationships in just the same way as if you were meeting them face-to-face.

When to use online or face-to-face networking

Everyone should use a mix of online or face-to-face networking within their networking strategy. (In Part 4 of this book, we show you how to put together your own networking strategy.) However, there will always be times when it is more effective to focus more on one or the other. Let's illustrate this with four examples.

Raj sells high-value and complex engineering services. The buyers of his service are normally directors and senior managers within the public sector, who tend not to be regular online networkers. Raj is more likely to meet these people if he focuses more of his time on face-to-face networking rather than online networking. Raj uses his online networking time, mostly on LinkedIn, to stay in touch with his network, but also to find potential suppliers and employees for his business.

---

[5] Clapperton, G., *This is Social Media: Tweet, blog, link and post your way to business success*, Capstone, 2009.

Jane is a lawyer who specialises in working with mothers who run their own business, 'mumpreneurs'. As 'mumpreneurs' are heavy users of online networking, Jane focuses the majority of her networking time on Twitter and internet forums aimed at female entrepreneurs. Jane is very selective with her face-to-face networking and spends her face-to-face networking time at conferences aimed at 'mumpreneurs'. She uses her time at the conferences to strengthen her relationships with her online business contacts by spending time with them in person.

Clint wants to relocate from London to Edinburgh to be closer to his family. He wants a new role within the audit department of a mid-sized accountancy practice. His current practice does not have a presence within Scotland so he is looking for a new employer. He uses LinkedIn to 'meet' auditors and recruitment managers from Edinburgh-based firms. Once he has 'met' a useful contact on LinkedIn, he aims to set up a phone call to get to know them better.

Sarah works for an international management consultancy at their London headquarters. She is ambitious and wants to make partner within her current firm. She is aware that to achieve her career ambitions and get the right assignments, she needs an extensive network and 'good' profile within the firm. She focuses her networking time attending internal firm events and volunteering for cross-firm assignments, projects and committees. She uses Facebook to strengthen the relationships she has with the people she works with.

As you can see, there is no one-size-fits-all answer. To decide on the right balance between online and face-to-face networking for your particular business and career goals, you need to ask yourself the following questions:

1 What am I trying to achieve with my networking strategy? New business? New job? New team members? Relationships with new suppliers?

2 Where do people well connected to the people I want to meet (e.g. introducers) spend their time, both physically and virtually?

3 How IT literate are the people well connected to my target market?

4 How much time in my personal and professional life do I have to attend regular face-to-face informal and formal networking events?

5 Where are the people I want to meet located and how easily can I spend time in that location?

6 Do I need to be able to meet people face-to-face before I can achieve my networking objective?

7 How can I use online networking to complement my face-to-face networking?

Summary

Networking is the process by which we choose to meet people and interact with them. Without realising it, most of us are consistently networking throughout our waking hours. Effective business networking is the process of building up mutually beneficial relationships for your career or business.

Professionals fundamentally network for four reasons:

1 To improve their profile, i.e. being 'found'.

2 To generate opportunities such as a new job or new clients.

3 To extend and strengthen the community around them.

4 To find answers and 'tools'.

You have a choice about how much time you will spend networking, by what means you will network, and how much success you will generate for yourself when networking.

Professionals who are keen for career and business success can no longer afford to ignore online networking. Online networking is being used successfully by professionals of all ages and levels of expertise to find new clients and jobs.

In reality, most face-to-face networking is about people standing around and talking to each other. Online networking is no different. It's how well you do this 'standing around and talking', whether face-to-face or online, that will determine your success as a networker.

Use online social networking sites such as Twitter and LinkedIn to widen your reach and keep in contact with a large network. Use face-to-face networking to strengthen and personalise relationships with people important to your career and business.

There is no one-size-fits-all answer for how much online versus face-to-face networking you should do. Only you personally can find the right balance between online and face-to-face networking to help you achieve your personal aims and objectives.

ACTION POINTS

■ Would you call yourself a proactive or passive networker? What could you start to do to become a proactive networker?

■ If you are avoiding networking, what's stopping you from networking? How could networking benefit you personally?

■ What personal goals or objectives do you have that your network could help you achieve?

■ Find a mentor skilled in both online and face-to-face networking who can help guide you to become a successful networker.

■ Identify how you can include online networking and face-to-face networking within your networking strategy.

■ Sign up to LinkedIn and join 'The Financial Times Guide to Business Networking' group on LinkedIn.

■ Find someone in your network who is successful at online and/or face-to-face networking and learn how they use online and/or face-to-face networking to help achieve their career and business aims.

■ If you don't enjoy networking, what's stopping you from enjoying it? What could you do to start enjoying networking?

Further resources

Books

Burton, B., *Get Off Your Arse*, 4Publishing, 2009.

D'Souza, S., *Brilliant Networking: What the best networkers know, do and say*, Prentice Hall, 2nd edn, 2010.

Lindenfield, G. and Lindenfield, S., *Confident Networking for Career Success and Satisfaction*, Piatkus Books, 2010.

Blogs

Joined Up Business Networking www.joinedupnetworking.com

2

How to create opportunities via networking

What topics are covered in this chapter?

- The four ingredients needed to consistently generate opportunities via networking
- How to generate these four ingredients within your networking strategy
- How to calculate your opportunity score

In the last chapter you learned what an effective networking strategy can do for your business and career, particularly if you combine your online and offline activities. As we stated, the skills, behaviours and attitude you need to make it work are complementary in both the virtual and real worlds – the same rules apply. This chapter gives you the four ingredients needed for effective networking activity.

1 *Credibility*. Before someone is willing to recommend you to someone in their network, they need to know that you are credible and reliable – a trustworthy referral. How do your actions and what you communicate impact on your credibility?

2 *Personal brand*. Networking is personal – it's about you, your 'brand' and how you communicate your brand to others. How do you present yourself to the world? How do you differentiate yourself from your competitors? How do you make yourself memorable? If someone Googles your name, what do they find? When they meet you at an event, what do you say?

3 *Visibility*. With people's networks increasing rapidly in size, how do you get to be that trusted person whom your network remembers and introduces to others?

4 *Social capital*. People help out others in their network because they want to. What do you need to do to get your network to actively help you?

In this chapter we show you a simple way to measure your performance in each of these four ingredients. The rest of the book will show you how to improve your skills and performance in each of these areas to become a successful networker.

The four ingredients needed to consistently generate opportunities via networking

Whilst it is impossible to predict where your next opportunity will come from via your networking activities, it is possible to improve the likelihood of generating opportunities via your network.

The likelihood of opportunities, i.e. referrals and recommendations, that you attract as a networker can be defined by the following equation:

$$Opportunity = Credibility \times (Personal\ brand + Visibility + Social\ capital)$$

where:

Opportunity represents an opportunity score – the greater this number, the higher the likelihood of opportunities coming to you

Credibility = your personal credibility

Personal brand = the marketability and strength of your personal brand

Visibility = visibility to your target market

Social capital = the amount of social capital you have generated within your network.

Later on in the chapter we will show you how to calculate your opportunity score. Before we do this, we will look in detail at the four ingredients for successful networking: credibility, personal brand, visibility and social capital.

1 Credibility

'It is about the afters. People don't give a damn about how fantastic you are, what reports you have, and if you phone people back in half an hour. They want to know, at the end of the day, whether you will deliver on what you say you are going to do.'

Gina Wadsworth, partner at Contact Consultants and BNI director

❝Credibility is an intangible quality which is difficult to define accurately❞

Credibility is an intangible quality, which is difficult to define accurately as it means different things to different people. Personally, I define someone who is credible as a person who has developed a reputation as someone who 'walks the walk and talks the talk' *and* delivers on all their commitments. But Ivan Misner, founder of BNI, defines credibility as '*the quality of being reliable, worthy of confidence*'.[1]

Before someone is willing to risk their reputation by recommending you to someone within their network, they want to know that you are credible, i.e. committed, will conduct yourself appropriately and will be able to deliver on something they put you forward for.

Robin, a coach, had a friend called Steve who was a committee member of two local photographic clubs. Both clubs were small but had different kinds of members. One had a long, extensive history and an older membership; the other was much younger and had a good mix of ages. Steve was treasurer for one and secretary for the other 'because no one else would volunteer'. But holding committee posts in the two clubs was adversely affecting his credibility. You may be wondering why. His credibility was low because both clubs saw he had divided loyalties. Robin asked him, 'In your heart of hearts, what do you want to be doing?' Steve said, 'Taking good photos.' 'So, which club is going to provide you with the best stimulus for that?' 'The younger one.' 'So what are you going to do?' 'Resign from the other club!' Steve did that and his photos now are being critically acclaimed around the world. One photo has been viewed 21,000 times in its first few weeks on the internet.

Until you get the opportunity to actually win business or get an interview, like Steve at the photography clubs, your credibility is built up via the perception of your personal brand and your behaviour and attitudes. For example, if you want to be seen as 'credible' when networking, you need to:

---

[1] 'Moving from visibility to credibility', http://businessnetworking.com

- do what you say you are going to do, for example phone people when you say you are going to
- arrive on time to meetings and events
- share client and customer success stories and testimonials
- have business cards with your contact details, plus details of your professional associations and memberships, professional qualifications and any awards won
- keep your messages, both online and offline, consistent over time
- focus on building the relationship rather than selling
- find simple ways to help the person you are meeting, for example connecting them with someone in your network
- get introductions to people you want to meet from 'credible' people within your network
- look the part.

Tip

When searching for a new job, have a set of business cards printed, clearly showing your contact details and URLs of your LinkedIn profile, blog and online CV.

I found my first coaching client, who was not an employee of my old employers, as a direct result of a recommendation from a partner within my old firm. This trusted recommendation helped my credibility and was a key factor in the client's decision to first talk with me and subsequently hire me as his coach.

Make sure that, when you are out networking, you are focused on finding out 'who you know' rather than on the heinous crime of selling. There is nothing quite as damning for your credibility as a sign on your forehead that says 'I am desperate for business' or 'I am selling'.

Your credibility normally is tested after a networking event or after meeting someone. Why? Remember that your credibility is linked directly to your ability to 'walk the walk and talk the talk' *and* deliver on all your commitments. Potential clients or employers are always looking for someone who is keen and eager to work with them. It may be only something small, such as sending a short email saying you enjoyed meeting them, but the small, and often inconsequential, stuff is taken as evidence of how you may behave if they hired or employed you. I was amazed, when I started face-to-face networking in earnest, how few people actually did follow up after a networking event. On the basis of my personal experiences, I can promise you that a simple email or handwritten note stating how much you enjoyed meeting someone will make you stand out positively from your peers.

For example, I suggested to one of my clients, who was looking for a new job, that she sent a short email to her interviewers after her interview, saying thank you for their time and how much she enjoyed meeting them. The interviewers delayed their hiring decision as they couldn't decide between her and another candidate. In the end my client got the job without the need for a further interview. Did the follow-up email tip the balance for my client? In all honesty we will never know, but I bet it helped!

2 Personal brand

Why a strong personal brand is essential for networkers today

'The fundamental purpose of brands is to create loyalty and preference over the long term.'

Jez Frampton, global chief executive of Interbrand[2]

When people buy professional services, generally they are buying a high-value product, service or person. For this reason there has to be a high degree of trust between the buyer and seller before the purchase will take place. This means that a potential buyer of professional services will prefer to act on a referral or recommendation from someone they know, like and trust before engaging in a conversation with a potential supplier. If you are fortunate enough to be recommended, it means they are placing trust in you, not the company that employs you. It's your personal brand that they prefer rather than your employer's brand.

The recent rapid growth and adoption of social media has led to people being able to quickly generate a strong online personal brand and rapidly communicate their brand's promise via word-of-mouth referrals. Social media also is enabling people to maintain networks vastly bigger than a network based on face-to-face interactions alone. Whereas only five years ago we may have had only one or two people within our network whom we would have been happy to recommend, today we are only one click or Google search away from generating five or

❛❛Investing time and energy in building your personal brand is essential❜❜

---

[2] Interbrand report: *Best Global Brands 2013*, www.interbrand.com/en/best-global-brands/2013/Best-Global-Brands-2013.aspx

six recommendations of people within our network. It's the strength and marketability of our personal brand that is the determining factor as to whether we will be the person that others recommend. This is why investing time and energy in building your personal brand is essential to networkers today.

What is a personal brand?

'A personal brand states exactly what you can do, refers to you by your own name and carries with it the domain within which you operate.'

Robert Watson, Valuable Comment

A personal brand is made up of your personal vision and purpose, values, skills, knowledge, natural talents, beliefs and attitudes, i.e. your brand attributes and characteristics. However, when you think about hiring a person, you are not thinking about their vision or purpose but your perception of them, i.e. how they position themselves in your mind by the brand attributes they choose to display and communicate. For example, Sir Bob Geldof is *the* guy you go to when you have a *big* humanitarian cause needing *huge* efforts from people who aren't looking to profit from their contribution.

'Personal branding is the process where you figure out what makes you special and then communicate it to a specific audience.'

Dan Schawbel, author of Me 2.0: Build a powerful brand to achieve career success

There are four main ways that we position and package, i.e. communicate, our personal brand to people around us:

What you do

- ■ What service or product you provide.
- ■ The niche, sector or community within which you operate.

How you do it

- ■ What processes, systems, communication media you use.
- ■ Where you choose to spend time physically and virtually.

How you show yourself to the world

- ■ How you listen, e.g. are you truly listening or just waiting for a gap to get your point across?
- ■ How you choose to look and dress, e.g. dressing in a well-tailored suit forms an impression in someone's mind.

- How you conduct yourself in a social setting, e.g. your social airs and graces.
- The possessions you surround yourself with, e.g. your car, phone, laptop case.
- Your body language.
- The image you present online.
- How well you handle your emotions, particularly when under stress, i.e. your emotional maturity.

How you let the world know about what you do

- What you say, how you say it and how you sound saying it.
- How and what you write.
- How effortlessly you have embraced new technology, such as social networking sites.
- How much of your personal life and circumstances you choose to share.

Similar to a brand team deciding to reposition their brand, you can also reposition the perception of your personal brand. For example, when Margaret Thatcher was the UK leader of the opposition, she worked on her image, specifically her voice and screen image. Her advisors, who thought her voice sounded too shrill, suggested she undertake voice training to lower the pitch to make her sound more authoritative.

Tip

A great personal brand to cultivate as a networker is someone who is helpful, well connected and delivers on their promises.

Ideas and inspiration to help you strengthen your personal brand

Quick ways anyone can strengthen their personal brand

1 Circulate articles (linked to your personal brand) to your network.
2 Include links on your email and forum signatures to your online articles and blogs.
3 Look the part.
4 Do what you say you are going to do.
5 Be authentic and true to your values and passions.
6 Ask people close to you what your strengths and particular talents are.

Ideas to strengthen your brand within your own organisation

1   Opt for assignments and work that will showcase your strengths.

2   Volunteer for high-profile assignments.

3   Offer to deliver presentations both in-house and externally.

4   Ask for 360° feedback from influential partners and directors within your firm.

5   Spend time helping more junior members in the firm build their career.

6   Write articles for the in-house newsletter or blog.

7   Offer to become a mentor.

8   Get on an assignment that is being led by a known expert within your firm.

9   Routinely ask for feedback at the end of each assignment and share any positive feedback with people who have influence over your career.

Ideas to strengthen your personal brand outside your own organisation

1   Volunteer to be a guest speaker at networking groups and conferences.

2   Run training sessions and workshops on topics connected to your personal brand.

3   Find a mentor, outside your organisation, who is seen to be strong in the area in which you want to become famous.

4   Tweet about your area of specialism.

5   Have business cards printed with links to your online presence.

6   Record YouTube videos on subjects based around your personal brand.

7   Start a special interest group within your professional association.

8   Take a committee, moderator or board-level role within your professional association, special interest group or online forum.

9   Ask for testimonials and endorsements from experts within your field.

10 Register the domain name for your personal name and use it as your online CV.

How to use writing to strengthen your brand

1   Write articles for in-house publications, external magazines (print and online), newsletters or blogs.

2   Start a blog based around your personal brand.

3   Comment on blogs that are focused on your personal brand.

4   Submit articles to online article sites.

5   Write an eBook or book.

6   Start writing a column for an internal or external print/online magazine.

7   Participate in online forums and answer questions based around your specialism.

8   Interview well-known experts in your field for your blog.

9   Offer to guest blog for other people, particularly key influencers in your industry.

> **How to use LinkedIn to strengthen your brand**
> 1   Start a LinkedIn group that enables you to showcase your expertise.
> 2   Comment on LinkedIn discussions and status updates that showcase your expertise
> 3   Include presentations, videos, white papers and articles on your LinkedIn profile.

Adopting a niche

In recent years, people have become conditioned to expect that via the internet they can quickly find the answers, potential employee or supplier that they need to help them. If you want to be the chosen person, your personal brand needs to include a commitment to a specialism or working within a niche market. Any potential employer, client or customer will Google your name (or your company name) before they engage with you. If you haven't built up a credible online presence, which reinforces your personal brand, then you are likely to be missing out on opportunities.

3 Visibility

'Visibility is the point when someone becomes aware of the nature of your business.'

Ivan Misner, founder of BNI[3]

> **Tip**
> When you join a formal networking group such as BNI or 4Networking, ask to do the member spotlight feature early into your membership.

First, what do we mean by being visible? Someone I used to work with called it 'top-of-the-mind' visibility, i.e. when someone within your network sees or hears of an opportunity, you are the first person they think of. With online networking giving people more choice over who within their network to recommend or contact, it has become easier to gain visibility with more people but harder to maintain 'top-of-the-mind' visibility with the people who are more likely to help you achieve your career or business goals.

---

[3] 'The first stage of the VCP process, visibility', http://businessnetworking.com/moving-from-visibility-to-credibility/

To achieve 'top-of-the-mind' visibility, you could:

- be present regularly at local face-to-face networking events
- attend all the meetings of your formal networking club
- post on forums regularly
- update your status daily on social networking sites
- tweet regularly during the day
- send a regular newsletter to your network
- turn up to company formal and informal social events
- send articles of interest to your network regularly.

> **Tip**
>
> If you are new to an online forum, take the opportunity to introduce yourself to all the members of the forum. Normally there is a section or pre-existing conversation where new members introduce themselves to the rest of the forum members.

4 Social capital

'Ask not what your network can do for you, but what you can do for your network!'

Hamish Taylor, Shinergise Partners

Do you remember when you were at school and there was a boy or a girl who was incredibly popular? Everyone wanted to be their friend. These were the people who were always picked first for teams. Everyone seemed to know this boy or girl and, when they decided what they wanted to do, everyone seemed to want to do it with them. These people held great influence over the class. The most popular person at school had accumulated a large amount of what I am calling social capital.

" Social capital can be measured by the breadth and the depth of your network "

Social capital is the imaginary bank account that you build up by being helpful to people. Social capital can be measured by the breadth and the depth of your network, the strength of your relationships within that network, and the goodwill and level of influence you have within that network.

The extent of your personal reach and your level of influence within your network, i.e. your social capital, will be key factors in whether you generate the opportunities you want and need from your network.

How to increase your social capital

Similar to financial capital, social capital has to be earned and accumulated, but it can also be spent. The more deposits you make in your emotional bank balance with someone, the greater likelihood that your relationship will stay strong if you make a withdrawal later. It's the same with social capital – the more goodwill and influence you gain with your network, the greater the amount of social capital you are accumulating within your network.

> **Tip**
>
> To quickly increase your social capital, offer to take a position of responsibility within a committee, club or group to which you belong.

Your level of social capital is enhanced by who you know and who you are seen with. If you spend time with people who have a greater level of prestige, credibility or status, some of that automatically rubs off on you. Let's say you wanted to join a charity but you weren't especially tied to any one cause. You look around, and the local cancer support group has three prominent business leaders on the committee. Spending time with these three prominent business leaders will help you increase your social capital.

To earn and accumulate social capital takes time and investment on your part. The most successful networkers use behaviours and attitudes that automatically build up their social capital with the right people in their networks. In the next section of this chapter we will look at the behaviours and attitudes that successful networkers consistently demonstrate.

> **Twenty quick and easy ways to increase your social capital with people in your network**
>
> 1 Send a thank-you card or follow-up email after meeting them.
> 2 Call someone in your network.
> 3 Send a birthday, Christmas or 'well done' card.
> 4 Arrange a speaking engagement for them.
> 5 Make an introduction.
> 6 Pass on a referral.
> 7 Write a testimonial.
> 8 Write an article for them.
> 9 Post a blog written by them on your blog.
> 10 Put a link from your blog to their website or blog.

11 Connect with them on more than one social networking site.

12 Send an article of interest.

13 Nominate them for an award.

14 Vote for them in an award.

15 Send them a small gift.

16 Invite them to some corporate hospitality.

17 Include an article from them in your newsletter.

18 Help them with a query or question they have posted on a social networking site.

19 Have a one-to-one meeting with someone.

20 Bring along a guest to a networking meeting.

What one thing could you do today to increase your social capital within your network?

Measuring your opportunity score

As a general rule of thumb, the higher your opportunity score, the greater likelihood of success via networking. By measuring your opportunity score, you will be able to see easily where to place your effort to increase the number of opportunities you attract via your networking activities.

To measure your current opportunity score, look at Table 2.1 and score yourself between 1 and 5 for each of the 4 ingredients for successful networking: credibility, personal brand, visibility and social capital.

Table 2.1 Calculating your personal opportunity score

Score	Personal brand	Visibility	Social capital	Credibility
	The marketability and strength of your personal brand	*Your profile amongst your target market*	*The influence and reach you have within your network*	*The extent to which you deliver on your promises and 'walk your walk' and 'talk your talk'*
1	You are not distinguishable amongst your peers	Your target market has never heard of you	Influential only amongst relatives and immediate work colleagues	You have no track record in your specialist area and are unlikely to write or talk about your specialist subject
2	You are known amongst your close network as 'the person' to talk to for 'y'	Your target market becomes aware of you	Strong influence on up to 50 people	You may write or talk about your specialist subject. Some people ask your opinion, but often they are asking others ahead of you

Score	Personal brand	Visibility	Social capital	Credibility
	The marketability and strength of your personal brand	*Your profile amongst your target market*	*The influence and reach you have within your network*	*The extent to which you deliver on your promises and 'walk your walk' and 'talk your talk'*
3	You have an active social media presence and are known amongst your wide network as 'the person' to talk to for 'y'	Your name is known within your target market and you may have a small following on social media (<1,000 followers)	Strong influence on 51 to 150 people	You write and talk regularly about your specialist subject and are building up a small client list
4	You may have a book published and have a very active social media presence – via blogging and social networking sites. Journalists occasionally will quote you. Your personal brand is now becoming stronger than your business's brand	Your name is well known within your target market and you are likely to have a medium-sized following (2,000 followers or connections) on social media	Strong influence on 151 to 500 people	You write and talk regularly about your specialist subject and have a well-stocked client list, with a few people using you as a trusted advisor
5	You have written books, published articles, appeared on TV, presented at major conferences and are a household name within your industry or area of specialism	Your name is widely known within your target market and you are likely to have a large following (10,000 followers or connections) on social media	Strong influence on more than 501 people	You are in constant demand to write and talk about your specialist subject. You have an impressive client list and there are many people who use you as a trusted advisor

Let's take a worked example. One of my business coaching clients, an HR consultant, wanted to increase significantly the number of referrals she generated via her networking activities. We calculated her opportunity score, using Table 2.1, and this was how she scored:

Personal brand	2
Credibility	2
Visibility	2
Social capital	3
Opportunity score *(Credibility × (Personal brand + Visibility + Social capital)*	14

❝You will gain ideas and inspiration to improve your own opportunity score❞

After calculating her opportunity score, my client decided to focus her networking efforts to increase her credibility with her target audience. Six months later, her investment to increase her credibility with her target audience had paid off: her word-of-mouth referrals and recommendations had doubled.

As you read through this book, you will gain ideas and inspiration to improve your own opportunity score and become a more effective networker.

Summary

There are four ingredients needed for networking success:

■ credibility – the extent to which you deliver on your promises and 'walk your walk' and 'talk your talk'

■ personal branding – the marketability and strength of your personal brand

■ visibility – your profile amongst your target market

■ social capital – the influence and reach you have within your network.

Before someone is willing to risk their reputation by recommending you to someone within their network, they want to know that you are credible, i.e. committed, will conduct yourself appropriately and will be able to deliver on something they put you forward for.

A potential buyer of professional services will prefer to act on a referral or recommendation from someone they know, like and trust before engaging in a conversation with a potential supplier. As people's networks increase significantly in size due to the extra reach afforded to them by social networking, the strength of your personal brand will be a significant contributory factor in whether they contact you first.

Your personal brand attributes are your vision and purpose, values, skills, knowledge, natural talents, beliefs and attitudes. You position your personal brand in the minds of others by how, when and where you choose to communicate to others.

With online networking giving people more choice over who within their network to recommend or contact, it has become easier to gain visibility with more people but harder to maintain 'top-of-the-mind' visibility with the people who are more likely to help you achieve your career or business goals.

The extent of your personal reach and your level of influence within your network, i.e. your social capital, will be key factors in whether you generate the opportunities you want and need from your network.

By measuring and knowing your opportunity score, you know where best to expend your efforts to generate success via your networking activities.

ACTION POINTS

■ Identify the 10 people who could have a positive impact on your business or career. Assess the amount of social capital you have with these 10 people (low, medium or high). For anyone with whom you have low or medium social capital, identify ways to increase your social capital with them.

■ Ask three people close to you what you could do to increase the influence within your personal network.

■ Identify three ways in which you can increase and maintain your 'top-of-the-mind' visibility with people important to your career and business success.

■ Research where people who are important to your career or business success maintain an online presence.

■ Start writing articles for a magazine, blog or newsletter on topics based around your personal brand.

■ Identify three ways in which you may be damaging your credibility. Now commit to an action to change your behaviour.

■ After you have met someone, get into the habit of sending them a short email stating how much you enjoyed meeting them and asking them to connect with you on LinkedIn, Twitter and other social networks.

■ Ask your mentor or manager, or people you trust, for feedback on how visible and credible you are to senior managers, directors and partners within your firm.

■ Calculate your opportunity score and identify three simple ways in which you can increase your score.

Further resources

Books

D'Souza, S., *Brilliant Networking: What the best networkers know, do and say*, Prentice Hall, 2nd edn, 2010.

Lindenfield, G. and Lindenfield, S., *Confident Networking for Career Success and Satisfaction*, Piatkus Books, 2010.

Misner, I.R., Alexander, D.C. and Hilliard, B., *Networking Like a Pro: Turning contacts into connections*, Entrepreneur Press, 2010.

Schawbel, D., *Me 2.0: Build a powerful brand to achieve career success*, Kaplan Trade, revised edn, 2010.

Blogs and websites

Rob Brown's blog www.therobbrown.com/connected-professional/

Business Networking Blog http://www.business-networking.co.uk

Joined Up Business Networking for Professionals http://joinedupnetworking.com

Andy Lopata's 'Connecting is not enough' blog www.lopata.co.uk/blog

Ivan Misner's 'Networking Now' blog http://businessnetworking.com

Dan Schawbel's 'Personal Branding' blog www.personalbrandingblog.com

3

Behave like a great networker

What topics are covered in this chapter?

■ How to think and behave to gain success when networking

■ The right attitudes needed to become a great networker

In the previous chapter you learned about the four essential ingredients needed to be successful at networking. But if you are going to build your credibility, visibility, social capital and personal brand you've got to behave and think appropriately. Networking with the right attitude is key – don't think of it as selling, although it may generate you sales or a new job, ultimately. If you go in with a selling attitude, it will put off people wanting to develop a relationship with you. This chapter shows you how the right behaviours and attitudes will lead you to networking success. Here we will look at 14 ways in which great networkers think and behave:

1   Be selfless and generous.

2   Be 'always open for networking'.

3   Be interested in people first and foremost, business second.

4   Be positive and enthusiastic.

5   Be focused and disciplined.

6   Cultivate a win–win mentality.

7   Be brave.

8   Be committed.

9   Be willing to experiment.

10   Be curious.

11   Be tenacious and persistent.

12   Be authentic.

13   Seek first to understand.

14   Act like the host.

1 Be selfless and generous

'The purpose of networking is to find out how you can help people and then help them.'

Jeremy Marchant, Emotional Intelligence at Work[1]

> The guiding principle of BNI, the world's largest business networking organisation, is Givers Gain®: the good you do comes back to you over the long term and often in indirect ways.

Good networkers believe in something called abundance, i.e. there is always enough to go around. Very often business people and job hunters believe the opposite is true, i.e. they assume that there is only a limited amount of business and jobs to go around. This can lead to competitive and aggressive behaviour, which damages credibility, reduces social capital and literally stifles opportunities from networking activities.

The abundance mindset generates opportunities due to the 'law of reciprocity'. Robert Cialdini, in his book *Influence: The Psychology of Persuasion*, identified the 'law of reciprocity', i.e. that people are more likely to reciprocate if you do something positive for them first.[2] Be aware that successful networkers, such as Jonathan Senior, managing director of Sharp End Training (www.sharp-end-training.co.uk), who offered to host my new website for free, don't apply the law of reciprocity in a calculating way – it's not about expecting a quid pro quo. They know that, if they help someone out, they will benefit at some point in a roundabout way – it just may not be directly from the person they helped out.

[1]   www.emotionalintelligenceatwork.com
[2]   Cialdini, R., *Influence: The Psychology of Persuasion*, 1st Collins Business Essentials, revised edn, 2007.

2 Be 'always open for networking'

When I met Elinor Barbary in April 2010, her business was three months old and growing rapidly. Elinor is a great example of someone who is 'always open for networking'. Even though I was interviewing her for research for my book, Elinor directly gained two new clients as a result of the introductions I gave her after our conversation. Great networkers, like Elinor, don't see any boundaries between their personal and professional lives, or online and face-to-face networking. They are literally always looking for opportunities to network and help someone. In the past six months, I've embraced this 'always open for networking' within my personal life. Like many parents with young children, I found attending birthday parties with my children a chore. I decided to view these parties as an opportunity to meet some interesting people. As a direct result of this mindset change, I've recently met some new associates for The Excedia Group and potential clients when attending birthday parties and social events with my children.

> **Tip**
>
> Always have your business card with you. You never know when you may need it.

3 Be interested in people first and foremost, business second

" Good networkers know that networking is not about selling "

How many times have you been at an event and been pitched to? How did it feel? I bet you were thinking, how do I end this conversation and move on? Everyone hates being sold to. If you find yourself trying to convince someone to take up an opportunity, even a free opportunity, this is selling. Good networkers know that networking is not about selling, it's about getting to know people.

> **Tip**
>
> When meeting someone for the first time at a networking event, make sure you don't ask them first: 'What do you do?', as this gives the impression that you are interested only in what you can sell to them. Instead, ask them a question that shows an interest in them as a person, such as: 'How's your week going?'

The questions that you use when meeting someone for the first time often will demonstrate to the person whether you are interested in them or their business. When you meet someone for the first time (unless they have called a sales meeting specifically), either online or in person, it is not the time or place to be using questions to qualify how ready they are to do business with you or whether they have a vacancy. This is selling, not networking.

Good questions that demonstrate your interest in them as a person could include:

- How long have you been in business?
- Tell me your story of how you came to be your own boss/in your current role/looking for a new role.
- How long have you been in your current role?
- What do you like about running your own business?
- What do you like about your current role or current employer?
- What prompted you to be your own boss?
- What prompted you to pursue a career as a...?
- What is your ideal or typical client?
- What are you looking to achieve at this event?
- If you could change one thing about your business/job, what would that be?
- When you are not working, what do you enjoy doing?

4 Be positive and enthusiastic

The best networkers attract people towards them, and they are the sort of people you enjoy spending time with. I found that the great networkers I spoke to in my research tended to be upbeat, positive and generally enthusiastic about the future and what it held for them. As a result, it was easy to spend time getting to know them. Positivity and enthusiasm help to build up your social capital. The flipside is that negative, apathetic and critical people tend to act like a drain on our emotions and energy, which leads to a reduction in their social capital. Who would you like to spend your time with, someone you feel good with or someone who drains the positive energy out of you?

5 Be focused and disciplined

Great networkers, like Babs Morse, an image consultant, love meeting and spending time with people. Babs learned the hard way that she needed to be focused when out networking. Too much networking without a purpose, whilst enjoyable, was costing her time and business. Babs now limits her networking to networking groups with a high percentage of her target market. She systematically tracks all her referrals and recommendations back to the source and networking group. Babs uses a simple spreadsheet to capture all her data on referrals; however, your customer relationship management (CRM) system may do this for you. She then uses this information to make decisions on whether to renew her annual membership to the six networking groups of which she is a member.

Tip

Pick a maximum of three internet forums in which to maintain a presence. Any more and you will spread yourself too thinly.

This takes discipline, and often a sizeable investment in time, processes and systems. Set yourself goals and targets similar to Bryony Thomas, author of *Watertight Marketing*. Bryony has a monthly handshake quota of 10 people, i.e. within a month she will meet physically at least 10 people who will benefit her or her business. How easy would it be for you to aim to meet one or two new people a month?

It's this focus and discipline that enables the best networkers to maintain an effective level of visibility at the forums, social networking sites and networking groups they frequent.

Tip

Eighty per cent of success from networking comes not from meeting new people but from maintaining contact with your existing network.

6 Cultivate a win–win mentality

When I started out in business, I was given my first freelance opportunity by Alan Smith, of Alan Smith & Associates. I had met Alan first when he had run a team day for one of my internal client groups. Alan had asked to stay in touch (always the sign of a good networker!). As Alan's firm special-ised in outplacement and career coaching, he was one of the first people I talked to when I realised I was becoming self-employed. I was interested to know what qualifications and experience I needed to work as a career coach in the outplacement sector. What started as a fact-finding conversation soon ended up as a hiring conversation, as Alan realised that I could help him out with one of his legal clients who wanted to do some leadership development work. When it dawned on me that Alan had a job in mind for me, I then introduced him to John Stylianou, one of my team members at the time, who was also leaving to become self-employed. This win–win mentality worked incredibly well in the short, medium and long term for Alan, John and myself. Both John and I gained this, and subsequent, work from the conversation, and have worked together closely ever since. Alan ended up winning from the conversation, as he gained a team of learning and development specialists with credibility within professional services, to complement his firm's growing specialism in outplacement for professional services.

Networking works best when the people you are networking with have a collaboration mindset, i.e. they are always looking for the win–win. It's linked back to the abundance principle. If you truly believe that there is enough business (or jobs) to go around, you are always looking for a win–win outcome for the people within your network.

7 Be brave

'I don't have any qualms about dropping an email or a LinkedIn request to somebody who is quite high profile within my sort of industry. And, as a result of that, I have made very strong links with high-profile and influential people in my industry.'

Karen Spillane, training professional

> **Tip**
>
> If you want a highly influential member of your firm or business to be your mentor, just ask, and tell them why you have chosen them. Most people are flattered to be asked and will say 'yes'.

As we grow up, we learn social etiquette but also form perceptions of people based on their position, perceived authority and experience. We can often

❝Great networkers see only the person, not the title❞

fall into the trap of seeing the title rather than the person. Most conference speakers and industry experts are very willing to have a conversation with anyone who asks them. If you find yourself saying or thinking, 'I couldn't talk to them because... ', take a moment to think whether a young child would see any barrier to a conversation. If a young child wouldn't see a barrier, then you are applying an imaginary barrier, i.e. letting a self-limiting belief reduce the size and effectiveness of your network. Everyone I interviewed for this book either self-selected themselves or readily made themselves available for an interview, regardless of their time zone, title or expert status. All I had to do was pluck up the courage to ask.

Great networkers see only the person, not the title, and are always brave enough to have the conversation that will make a difference to their career or business.

8 Be committed

Jon Baker, my business partner, and I were looking through our LinkedIn contacts for a new accountant. As we were discussing suitable candidates, one of the main criteria for selection was commitment. How likely were they to follow through on their commitments?

When someone recommends you or gives you a referral, they are placing their reputation on the line for you. To risk their reputation or credibility for you, they want to know that you are committed for the foreseeable future to what you are doing, whether continuing within employment or your business's strategy and offering.

9 Be willing to experiment

The only things that are certain in life are change and uncertainty: businesses grow or decline; people move jobs; networking groups change. New networking groups, events and social networking sites are springing up all the time. This means that new opportunities to network always will be just around the corner. It's this willingness to experiment that means that the great networkers always seem to know where to spend their time to get the best return on their efforts.

10 Be curious

'I have an insatiable curiosity about people and business.'

Melissa Kidd, networking coach and trainer

The best networkers are inherently curious. They are curious about people, businesses and new experiences. This inbuilt curiosity helps them to seek out opportunities, for example new networking groups or sites, for themselves and others in their network, but also to find areas of common ground to build rapport with people they meet.

11 Be tenacious and persistent

Many people make the mistake of starting to invest in their network at the point at which they need it, such as at the start of a job hunt. I normally know when any of my ex-colleagues is thinking of leaving my old employer, as they get back in touch with me! Good networkers are investing in their network all the time, rather than waiting until they need to call upon their network. Think of your network as a fruit tree. Similar to a network, a fruit tree starts from a seed and then branches out as it grows. A good fruit tree bears fruit year after year only if it is looked after and nurtured. A fruit tree often takes a minimum of three years before it will produce a large harvestable crop year on year. Before a tree has reached maturity, you will be disappointed if you wish to enjoy the 'fruits of your labour'. As with a fruit tree, your network needs time to grow and mature. It will bear fruits – referrals, opportunities and recommendations – only if you take the time to maintain and nurture it. This is why the best networkers are tenacious and persistent. Great networkers know that, if they take the time to maintain and nurture their network, eventually it will bear fruit consistently.

12 Be authentic

As Dan Schawbel says in his book on personal branding, *Me 2.0*, your relationships, and therefore your social capital, depend on your authenticity.[3] Great networkers achieve their results on the back of building up strong and 'real' relationships with the people they meet. This means that the more authentic you can be with the people you meet, the more likely it is that you will generate mutually beneficial relationships.

---

[3] Schawbel, D., *Me 2.0: Build a powerful brand to achieve career success*, Kaplan Trade, 2010.

13 Seek first to understand

Gina Wadsworth, partner at Contact Consultants, an IT support business, is a director of three BNI groups and a member of a fourth. In the three groups she runs she does not talk openly about her business. However, because she always takes the time to listen, get to know and understand the members of her groups, she gains referrals still from all four groups, regardless of the role she plays in the group. This is no accident – consistent opportunities come through a network only when relationships have been built. After a while, the members Gina has spent time with truly to understand their business reciprocate and are genuinely interested in Gina's business. This investment of time to listen and understand others is part of the reason why Gina's business, via a marketing strategy built solely on networking, has doubled its profits and turnover every year for the past four years.

In Chapter 9 we will look in detail at how you can quickly develop rapport and build strong relationships with the people you meet when networking.

14 Act like the host

❝ Great networkers seem to have no fear ❞

When you are at a networking event, be it in person or virtual, you can choose to wait to be introduced or take the initiative and do the introducing. Social networks now are so big that normally it is ineffective to wait to be introduced. Great networkers seem to have no fear and take the initiative and introduce themselves to the people they want to meet. For example, if you are at a social event, don't wait for your host to introduce you to people, introduce yourself to the other guests. For more advice on 'working the room', see Part 3 of this book.

Summary

The best networkers use these behaviours and attitudes to build their social capital, visibility and credibility:

- Be selfless and generous.
- Be always open for networking – no boundaries between personal and professional life, or online and face-to-face networking.
- Be interested in people first and foremost, business second.
- Be positive and enthusiastic.

■ Be focused and disciplined.

■ Cultivate a win–win mentality.

■ Be brave.

■ Be committed.

■ Be willing to experiment.

■ Be curious.

■ Be tenacious and persistent.

■ Be authentic.

■ Seek first to understand.

■ Act like the host.

ACTION POINTS

■ Look at the list of 14 ways in which great networkers think and behave. What are your top three strengths in this list? What are your three greatest weaknesses in this list? What can you do to improve on your weaknesses?

■ The next time you meet someone for the first time, take the time to listen to them and find out as much as you can about them. Notice how this conversation differs from your normal 'first' conversations.

■ Where can you use your personal network to help you achieve business or career success?

■ Look through your personal and professional network and find three people who would benefit from introductions to other people in your network.

■ Who would be your first-choice mentor? What's stopping you from asking them?

■ Look through your network, in particular the people who are most important to your business or career. How much do you really know about them as a person? Next time you see or talk to one of these people, take the time to find out more about them as a person.

■ Outside of your working life, identify where you have some opportunities to network informally.

■ Think about your personal circumstances and decide on a target number of new people and existing members of your network to contact or meet each month.

Further resources

Books

Burton, B., *Get Off Your Arse*, 4Publishing, 2009.

Cialdini, R., *Influence: The psychology of persuasion*, 1st Collins Business Essentials, revised edn, 2007.

D'Souza, S., *Brilliant Networking: What the best networkers know, do and say*, Prentice Hall, 2nd edn, 2010.

Lindenfield, G. and Lindenfield, S., *Confident Networking for Career Success and Satisfaction*, Piatkus Books, 2010.

Lopata, A. and Roper, P., *...And Death Came Third! The definitive guide to networking and speaking in public*, Ecademy Press, 2nd revised edn, 2011.

Blogs and websites

Joined Up Business Networking www.joinedupnetworking.com

Andy Lopata's 'Connecting is not enough' blog www.lopata.co.uk/blog

Ivan Misner's blog http://businessnetworking.com

2

Online and face-to-face networking options explored

'In terms of business networking groups, I look at networks and I say they achieve one of four things. They are either there to increase your profile, build your community, help you equip yourself better or help you generate referrals.'

Andy Lopata, co-author of ...And Death Came Third!

There are a myriad of face-to-face and online networking options available to the professional today. However, when you are networking, you are doing one or more of the following things:

- increasing your profile
- helping you learn, find answers and tools to your problems
- generating referrals
- assisting you to build a community of like-minded people.

In the next three chapters we are going to look at all the different networking options available to you and how you can maximise your effectiveness in all four of the above at each different type of event.

In 'Further resources' at the end of the book there is a section with contact details of major face-to-face and online networking groups.

4

Face-to-face options

What topics are covered in this chapter?

- Where and when you should network in person
- How to maximise your effectiveness at a face-to-face networking event
- The pros and cons of each different type of face-to-face networking event

By the end of this chapter you will learn where you should network in person and how to maximise your effectiveness when networking in person.

You can network literally any time and anywhere. Very simply, you need only one other person to talk to in order to be able to indulge in some face-to-face networking. Face-to-face networking is wider than just attending a formal networking event. For example, these are all places where you can network:

- formal networking groups
- business clubs
- parent-friendly networking clubs
- professional association events
- drop-in events
- conferences
- training courses
- award evenings
- speed networking events

- job seekers' clubs
- mastermind groups
- community-related causes
- volunteering
- personal social events
- company social events
- chance meetings
- corporate entertainment
- private members' clubs.

Events and networking groups designed to generate referrals

These include:

- formal networking groups and business clubs, e.g. BNI (www.bni.com) or 4Networking (www.4networking.biz)
- women-only formal networking clubs, e.g. Athena (http: theathenanetwork.co.uk) and Women In Business Network (www.wibn.co.uk).

What you can expect

In every town (and often village) in the UK there will be at least one business or networking club, which exists to help the members of the club form a referral network. Typically, a formal business networking group should yield a return on investment of at least 20 times the money you have paid to attend the group. It's no surprise then, that networking and business clubs, catering to the needs of the small business owner, are everywhere you look.

These are small to medium-sized groups that meet regularly – some as often as once a week, others as infrequently as once a month. The meetings generally will last a couple of hours and mostly take place over breakfast or lunch.

The meetings normally are very structured and focused on referral generation. Typically, a meeting will comprise informal networking, a spotlight feature on one member's business and a round of elevator pitches. Normally each member will stand up and do a short pitch about their business and what help they are looking for from the group. These pitches are known often as a '60 second', 'monthly minute' or '40-second slot'. In Chapter 8, we talk about your pitch in more detail.

'It is not the person who you are sat in front of – they may not be able to afford your services. But they may know many people who can afford and want your services. That is the bit that most people miss when networking. Your aim is to connect with their network, not try to sell to them.'

Brad Burton, founder of 4Networking

Most of these groups charge an annual subscription as well as a small fee for each meeting. Expect to pay £500–£1,000 per year for membership and meeting fees for one of these groups, although groups normally will allow you to attend as a visitor twice without having to join formally.

❝Many of these groups have a profession exclusivity policy❞ Many of these groups have a profession exclusivity policy – i.e. only one accountant, solicitor, business coach is allowed per group. Group members are expected to attend every meeting – or send a substitute in their place. Typically, the formal networking clubs and groups attract predominantly sole traders, micro-business owners and small businesses.

What's the benefit of attending a referral generation group?

'Being active in BNI is like having up to 40 sales people working for you, because your fellow members will be carrying your cards and referring your business to people they meet, without you having to pay them any salaries or commission.'

www.bni-europe.com/uk/bni-experience.php

These groups allow members to pool their resources, share their networks and become advocates and unpaid sales people for each other. Think how much more business you would gain with 10 extra sales people generating trusted referrals for your business.

'Seventy per cent of all my new clients in my first six months of business came via my membership of Athena.'

Alicia Cowan[1]

---

[1] www.aliciacowan.com

As well as the primary benefit of generating word-of-mouth business, a referral generation group often can be a good source of support and encouragement.

What are the downsides of attending a referral generation group?

Success in a referral generation group relies on group members being well connected to your target market and being prepared to invest time generating opportunities for you. When you join a group, these two conditions are not guaranteed.

Many of these groups take place early in the morning – which excludes membership from parents with early morning childcare responsibilities. For example, I attended a 'Business 4 Breakfast' group which met at 06:45 (this sort of start time is very common for breakfast networking clubs). Like many people, I was never at my best at this time in the morning, having woken at 05:45. Although, in the last few years, there are many more of these groups meeting at more parent-friendly times.

To generate a steady stream of referrals from your referral generation group, attendance at every meeting is vital. When you add up both the membership and meeting fees, plus the cost of your time to attend the meetings and have regular one-to-one meetings with the members, a referral generation group is a sizeable investment in your business.

Many of these groups are very structured and governed by many rules, practices and policies. Some people think that these rules often can hinder collaboration rather than encouraging it. If the pressure of continually having to provide leads for a group is simply too much for you, then it is probably time to leave the group.

How to maximise your effectiveness at a referral generation group

Ideally, your referral generation group should be made up of members who are well connected to your target market. Choose a group that seems to be the best fit for your personal style, intended market and your time availability.

When you are attending as a guest, gauge how much business is being passed at each meeting. Before joining a group, arrange to meet the chairperson of the group. Ask if they can show you the types of people who attend the meetings regularly. In my case, I am always interested in groups with accountants, lawyers and consultants.

Tip

Prepare your pitch in advance of the meeting. It's one less thing to remember to do before you set off for your group meeting.

Many people make the mistake of thinking that they will generate referrals and leads instantly when they join a referral generation group. You may be lucky, however the members of the group need to know, like and trust you before they will consistently pass business your way – particularly if you sell a complex or high-value product or service. Take the time to meet each and every member personally to build a strong relationship with them. As relationships take time to form, it will be months rather than weeks before the group will generate you referrals consistently.

case study   Liz

Liz was asked to join her local BNI group, as the previous accountant in the group had just left. As a result of her joining the group, she picked up over £15,000 worth of new clients in the first two months of being a member. There were two reasons for her early success. First, she was always very specific about the type of clients she wanted to meet. As a consequence, the other group members found it easy to introduce her to the right people in their networks. Second, she took the time to meet all the members of the group and find out about their business. As a result, she picked up a few clients from the existing group members.

BNI calls it Givers Gain® – this is the mindset that a successful networker always will be on the lookout for opportunities for others. If you have this mindset, then business follows almost always. The person within the group who works the hardest to find opportunities for the other members probably is also receiving the most opportunities passed their way.

It sounds slightly illogical but, the more specific you can be with your requests of the group, the more likely it is that members of the group will be able to help. For example, if you say, 'I am looking for local businesses that would like to save money', you are unlikely to get a response, as every business owner needs to save money. If you say, 'I am looking for local businesses that are looking to move premises and want to save money on their legal bills', you are more likely to get productive responses. See Chapter 8 for more on effective pitching at a networking event.

'Great sales stories are short, with a beginning, an end and no middle.'

Richard White, author of The Accidental Salesman®: Networking Survival Guide[2]

Prepare short stories of how your firm or business has helped its clients or customers. When you are new to a referral generation group, you need to focus on building up your credibility with the group; these sales stories will help build that credibility within the group. Your sales stories may highlight why people choose you, why people carry on choosing your firm, what you do to make sure you go the extra mile for your clients and customers, how much time/effort/money you have saved for your client...

❝**The sooner you can get this business spotlight, the better**❞

Most groups have a business spotlight feature. This is where one member gets the opportunity to showcase their business in more detail to the whole group. As a new member to the group, the sooner you can get this business spotlight, the better. Any opportunity to educate and inform group members about your business will take you nearer to your first referral from the group.

Generally, each referral generation group is 'run' by a few elected or unelected members. These members, or 'officers', often benefit from a reduced membership fee, as well as increased visibility from the membership of the group. The increased visibility, social capital and perceived level of trust, i.e. credibility, that is placed on the officers of the group tend to result in a higher level of referrals coming their way.

> **Tip**
>
> To get more people listening to your pitch, take the time to listen intently to their pitches.

When you join a referral generation group, first impressions are important. Consciously or subconsciously, the other members will be wondering

---

[2] White, R., *The Accidental Salesman®: Networking Survival Guide*, Book Shaker, 2011.

whether you will fit in and whether you will be an asset to the group. One of the best ways to help create a positive first impression and generate trust from the existing members is to listen to them and take a very active interest in them and their business. To quickly gain the trust of your fellow members, you need to put your business requirements and needs on the backburner. A good networker who has been talking about their business, will always then ask you how they can help you in your business.

To generate a referral from a member of the club, they need to have remembered you. This means you need to have achieved 'top-of-mind' visibility with them, i.e. when they hear about a problem or meet a client or contact, they think about you and how you could possibly help this person. For example, if you are a member of a business networking club that meets monthly, then if you miss one meeting it will be two months before you get an opportunity to see the rest of the club – this is more than enough time for a member to forget about you and your business.

Business networking clubs often can attract members from all different walks of life. Indeed, many business networking clubs have an 'exclusive' profession policy and allow only one member from one profession. The members of the club will not know your business as intimately as you do. Therefore, you need to educate the members on what problems you and your firm solve, and how to be able to spot the signs that someone needs your services and when to step in to offer assistance – that offer of assistance being, of course, to call you. For example, if you are a private-client solicitor whose practice has a conveyancing speciality, you need the members of the club to know that your firm is great at helping people who are thinking of moving house.

Guests can be a valuable source of referrals and business for all the members of the group. Take your time to ask people in your network to join you at your business networking meeting. This will build up your social capital with both your guests and the other members of the net-working club.

Tip

When a member sends a substitute to a meeting, take the opportunity to talk to them and get to know them. Substitutes tend to turn up only once to a group.

Events and networking opportunities designed to help increase your profile

These include:

■ company social events, e.g. employee leaving party, ad hoc drinks after work

■ speed networking events

■ award evenings

■ parent-friendly networking clubs

■ drop-in events, e.g. Chambers of Commerce networking events.

What you can expect

This type of networking involves mixing and mingling. Unlike formal networking clubs, normally there is only a light structure for the event. Sometimes these events may have a speech or presentation on a topic of interest to the participants at the event. Generally, although there are a few exceptions, these types of events don't tend to happen in the morning.

Parent-friendly networking clubs offer a way for parents who run their own business to network at a convenient time and place with other business owners. Typically, these organisations will offer a crèche facility so that, whilst you network, your child plays safely.

What are the benefits of attending profile-raising events?

Whilst formal networking clubs tend to attract small business owners and sole traders, potentially you could meet anyone from any business at these types of events. Your local Chambers of Commerce networking events could be attended by senior decision makers from local blue-chip companies as well as sole traders. Or the managing director could pop along to your colleague's leaving drinks. These types of networking events are some of the few places you can meet senior decision makers or people who wouldn't normally go out networking.

What are the downsides to attending these types of events?

These events rely on you being prepared to go and talk to people at the event. There is a skill in being able to 'work a room' (see Chapter 10).

❝Turning up to a networking event knowing no one takes bravery and courage❞

Turning up to a networking event knowing no one takes bravery and courage. This irrational fear of having to talk to people you don't know is one of the most common reasons why professionals dread going networking.

With these types of events the attendance list is often very fluid. Sometimes you can verify the events attendance list in advance – but very often organisers won't know who is or isn't attending. This makes it very difficult to be able to focus accurately your networking time and efforts.

At these events you may bump into the professional who has been told by the firm to go out and network to drum up some business. Very often these professionals have not been trained to network and will go out and try to sell their services to everyone they meet at these events. If you have ever been sold to whilst out networking, you will know how painful it is.

How to maximise your effectiveness at these types of events

At these events you never know who you are going to meet and who will suggest that 'we get together for a longer, more in-depth conversation'. If you have had a good conversation with someone, inevitably they will ask you for your business card and permission to stay in touch. Saying you 'don't have a business card', 'have run out' or 'forgotten your business cards' is unprofessional and will damage your credibility. If you are in the midst of a career change or don't get provided with business cards by your organisation, then get your own printed.

> **Tip**
> Keep a small stash of business cards in your handbag, car, laptop bag and coat pocket. That way you will never be without a business card.

If you turn up early, you have the opportunity to speak to people before the groups and closed conversations tend to form. I've noticed that the valuable conversations at networking events have a tendency to happen towards the end of the event. This is because there are fewer interruptions, everyone is more relaxed and people are less 'needy' to meet their quota of people.

'Before I attend any event, I will have identified and researched five people who I want to talk to at the event.'

Bryony Thomas, author of Watertight Marketing

> **Tip**
>
> Before you attend an event, ask around your social networks to see who else is attending.

Remember to prepare in advance of attending the event. For example:

- Ask your host for a guest list in advance.
- Identify three to six people you want to have a conversation with.
- Do some research on the contacts you want to meet – what line of business are they in? What particular business or personal challenges may they be facing?

On the day before you go to the networking event, have a quick look at some online news websites and relevant trade journals, and formulate an opinion on some of the top stories.

Now, Mr Smith from Fantastic Widgets may not be your target client. But he may know someone who is. If you want to stay in touch, then ask for his business card. But it is more powerful to find a reason to stay in touch. For example, 'Have you met so-and-so? I'll send you their details'; 'I was reading a great article – I will send you a copy'. This helps to build up your credibility and social capital with the person you have met.

In Chapter 3 we discussed how great networkers are focused and disciplined in their networking. Before you attend a profile-building event, always give yourself a goal or objective for the evening. For example, this could be 'talk to one person within my target market and get permission for a follow-up meeting'. This will help you make the most of any event you attend.

If there is someone on your list to meet at the event, ask your host to introduce you to them. It is very easy to get lost in a room full of people – and, if you are short like me, to be unable to spot the people you have come to meet. A good host normally will be very happy to make the introductions for you.

Events and networking to help you learn, find answers and tools for your problems

These include:

■ professional association events

■ mastermind groups

■ training courses

■ conferences and seminars

■ job seekers' clubs.

Professional association events

Professional associations often will host a series of events across the year, which will be of interest and benefit to their members. Most of these events are free or heavily subsidised for their members. For example, if your business plan involved you meeting accountants, have a look at the events hosted by the Association of Chartered Certified Accountants (ACCA). Members of professional associations may gain valuable continuing professional development (CPD) points as a result of attending their association's events. There is the opportunity to meet senior decision makers of medium- to large-sized companies at these events.

---

case study Nick

I met Nick at a CIMA event on networking. Nick was my host and I was the speaker for the event. Although, initially, there didn't seem to be any immediate benefit for staying in touch, we both enjoyed each other's company and conversation. As a result, we organised a face-to-face meeting and have met up regularly ever since. Over the last year we have helped each other out in many different ways. As a result of this relationship, we both have gained valuable insights and new clients.

Mastermind groups

These are groups of business owners who meet regularly to provide input, ideas and suggestions to help each other achieve their business goals. Most formal mastermind groups normally charge a fairly high monthly membership fee, coupled with an expectation that all members of the group will attend all the meetings. Often, mastermind groups are limited to one representative from each profession.

Training courses

These can be in-house or externally run training courses. Most training courses will include at least five people who are likely to be from a similar background to you. If you are on a residential course, it is a great way to make friends and strengthen relationships when you are bonding during your learning experiences.

Conferences and seminars

❝Conferences and seminars are a great place to meet like-minded professionals❞

Conferences and seminars are a great place to meet like-minded professionals – or find a large proportion of your target market in one place! They are a place where you can meet senior decision makers within micro, small, medium and large businesses. Normally, conferences involve a programme of keynote speakers and smaller workshops, and exhibitors (who have paid to be at the event!).

Job seekers' clubs

These are formal or informal clubs set up to help job seekers support and actively help each other in their quest to find a new job. Of job seekers who use a job club to help them find a new job, 84 per cent find success via this route.[3]

What are the benefits of attending events that help you learn, and give you answers and tools to solve your problems?

The obvious benefit of attending these types of events is the opportunity to learn and gain valuable continuing professional development credits. Five years ago, I attended a two-day residential leadership course run by my previous employers, BDO LLP. At this course I met one of the BDO LLP's partners, Wendy. We stayed in touch after the course and Wendy's

---

[3] Bolles, R.N., *What Colour is Your Parachute?*, Ten Speed Press, 2008.

recommendation led to my first private coaching client. These events, whilst directly helping you learn, are good for helping you raise your profile within your current organisation. Training courses and mastermind groups, due to the time spent with participants, are great for helping you develop strong relationships quickly.

These types of events, especially high-profile industry conferences, often contain a high proportion of your target market – including many senior-level decision makers. For example, a seminar by a firm of accountants for potential and existing clients always will be very well attended by partners.

Mastermind events are a great way for you to demonstrate your credibility and gain valuable social capital by freely sharing your expertise. These events often give you an intimate view of someone else's business, which often leads to business being generated for participants.

What are the downsides of attending these types of events?

Often these events are time hungry. For example, most mastermind groups will demand a day of your time each month. A training course or conference could take you out of the office and away from client work for two or three days. Most of these types of events will provide only short blocks of time for informal networking, as networking is not the prime purpose of the event.

How to maximise your effectiveness at an event to help you learn, find answers and tools for your problems

Speaking at conferences is a massive opportunity to build your personal brand and showcase your expertise. As a speaker at a conference, you are afforded a special status – making meeting influential people easier. Very often, your status as a speaker gives you instant credibility and social capital, meaning that attendees will go out of their way to talk to you and find out more about what you do. Often a speaker will get complimentary tickets to the conference. This is not always the case, as there are some trade shows, now disguised as conferences, where the speakers, delegates and exhibitors pay for the privilege of being there.

Unlike a profile-building event, these events will always have a guest list, which almost always is available before the event. If you have got the attendance list in advance, it eliminates the need to hide in a corner to check the attendee list. If the first time you see the attendee list is actually on the morning of the event, then you are already at a disadvantage to the experienced networker. Most conferences I have attended are noisy and heaving with people, and it takes many calls and text messages to find someone you have already agreed to meet up with – let alone bump into one of your targets.

Always ask for the delegate list in advance of the conference – most hosts normally are happy to provide this on request – and use LinkedIn and Google searches to find contact details for the people you want to meet. Most people who are contacted in advance by other conference delegates naturally are flattered at the attention and pleased to have someone to talk to.

The way of increasing the odds of having a good conversation with someone you want to meet is to contact them in advance of the event and arrange to meet over lunch, a coffee break or a session that neither of you wants to attend in the formal proceedings. Normally there is valuable networking time to be had before the formal part of the event starts and after the last formal session of the day. This is time when you could be arranging to meet people for a longer conversation. There is no reason why you have to stick slavishly to the formal agenda given to you at registration. Have you thought about organising your own dinner? Or hosting a discussion over lunch?

When you sit down for lunch, seminar, master class or presentation, you have a fabulous opportunity to strengthen the relationship with the person you are sitting next to. If you are on a training course, resist the temptation always to sit in the same place next to the same person. Push yourself out of your comfort zone and aim to sit next to a new person in each session. Try to avoid sitting with a colleague during a presentation or lunch – it is a waste of a good opportunity to bond with someone you've only just met. Five minutes before a formal session starts, ask your host to introduce you to one of the people you have come to the event to meet. You then simply say, 'I've enjoyed our conversation, may I join you?' If you've made the right impression, the answer normally will be 'Yes', and you now have a huge opportunity to build upon your initial conversation and develop a deeper relationship during the formal event proceedings.

Many people shy away from asking questions in sessions. Having been a guest speaker, I know that speakers want to be asked questions by the audience. There is nothing worse than finishing your presentation and no one asking a question! Asking insightful questions based around an area of your

> **"Remember to add people to your LinkedIn connections"**

expertise is a great way to get noticed by the entire audience. It also gives you something to talk about when someone comes up to you later and says, 'That was an interesting question you asked'. When asking your question, make sure you remember to state your name, business and what you do clearly.

Remember to send an email to all the people you have met at the event and follow up on your commitments to put some time in the diary to talk more. Remember to add people to your LinkedIn connections and start following them on Twitter.

Events and networking to help you build a personal community of like-minded people

These include:

■ community-related causes, e.g. rotary club

■ volunteering

■ social events

■ communal working groups, e.g. jelly groups

■ corporate entertainment

■ private members' clubs, e.g. One Alfred Place.

Community-related causes

These are groups of people who join together to support a community-related cause or shared mutual interest. These are normally good places to meet senior decision makers from medium- to large-sized companies who normally wouldn't be out networking. Examples of community-related cause groups are Rotary, residents' association, choir, book club, football club, etc.

Volunteering

Giving up some of your time to help in a charity or school, or to run the local branch of your professional association, is still a form of networking. If you are looking to meet senior decision makers from medium- to large-sized companies, then consider becoming a school governor or a trustee of a local charity.

Social events

These are events or get-togethers that happen within your social life. Friends' parties, children's play dates, family events are all places at which you can network and find opportunities.

Communal working groups

These are groups of people who meet up to work together, for example jelly groups (www.workatjelly.com). Whilst their primary purpose is to provide company for people who normally work alone, they are a great way to meet other small business owners and sole traders.

Corporate entertainment

This is where a supplier or client, or someone in the business world who wants to get to know you better, 'treats' you to a meal out, or a ticket to a cultural or sporting event. You could find yourself enjoying a seat in a box at the opera, or a corporate entertainment box at a football or rugby event.

Private members' clubs

These are places where like-minded people meet. Membership of these clubs normally is on a strict invitation-only basis, with rigorous vetting procedures for potential members. Your club membership is based often on your level of seniority, family status or personal connections.

What are the benefits of attending community-building events or groups?

These types of events, opportunities and places are a great way to network when you have no time to network, especially if you are using your network to help you find your next role.

What are the downsides to attending these types of events?

The primary purpose of this type of event is not networking. Each type of community-building event or occasion will have an implied social etiquette to which you will need to conform. Focusing too much on a person's business interests at a family event will make the other guests feel awkward and reduce your social capital.

How to maximise your effectiveness at an event to help you learn, find answers and tools for your problems

I'm sure we have all experienced formal social occasions where we know only a handful of people. At a typical wedding you will know fewer than half the guests and the other half are an unknown quantity. Remember to circulate at these events and, as well as potentially meeting some great new people, you will lessen the risk of getting stuck talking to your Great Auntie Mary. Setting yourself a goal or objective for these events will help to push you out of your comfort zone and circulate. If you have met someone at a social event who you would like to help you achieve your business or career goals, don't talk too much business at the event, book a follow-up conversation or meeting.

> **Remember to circulate at these events**

There are often strict, unstated cultural rules or etiquette at a social event or club. For example, men not wearing a jacket or tie at some of the private membership clubs in London may be refused entry. Find out from your host what rules or traditions you will be expected to observe at the event or occasion. Be aware that your host may have other things happening later in the day – or may want to get to bed early. Listen out for clues when it is time to leave – for example, your host yawning. Overstaying your welcome is a great way to reduce your social capital!

Summary

There are many different ways you can network in person:

- formal networking groups
- business clubs
- parent-friendly networking clubs
- professional association events
- drop-in events
- conferences
- training courses
- award evenings
- speed networking events
- job seekers' clubs
- mastermind groups

- community-related causes
- volunteering
- personal social events
- company social events
- chance meetings
- corporate entertainment
- private members' clubs.

To choose the right time and place to network in person, you need to answer the following questions:

- What's my primary purpose for going networking?
- How will this event, occasion or group help me achieve my career or business goals?
- How much time and energy can I invest in the club, group or occasion?

To maximise your effectiveness at the networking event, group or occasion:

- Always have your business cards with you.
- Make time for a follow-up conversation or email.
- Find a reason to stay in touch.
- Observe the social etiquette of the occasion or club and don't overstay your welcome.
- Give yourself goals for the event.
- Don't sell at an event – use an event to start and strengthen relationships.

ACTION POINTS

- Submit the following terms into Google: *xxxx + business networking*, where *xxxx* is the name of your local town, to find a list of networking groups that meet locally to you.
- Access your professional association's website and see what events it is hosting that you would enjoy and benefit from attending.
- Create your own or join a mastermind group.
- Commit to attend one face-to-face networking event in the next month. Before you attend the event, decide on your personal goal for the event.
- Find out where the 'rain-makers' in your firm and your competitors' firms spend their time networking in person.

■ Identify an organisation, outside of work, that you would enjoy spending time in to increase your personal network. For example, an arts, music or sports club, Rotary, Round Table, Lions, school governorship, charity, etc.

■ Update your status on Facebook, Twitter or LinkedIn before you go networking next to see who else is attending.

■ Next time you go to a networking event, request the attendance list in advance and make contact with three people at the event before you go.

Further resources

Books

Ferrazzi, K., *Never Eat Alone: And other secrets to success, one relationship at a time*, Crown Business, 2005 (expected updated 2nd edn June 2014).

Misner, I.R., Alexander, D.C. and Hilliard, B., *Networking Like a Pro: Turning contacts into connections*, Entrepreneur Press, 2010.

Websites and blogs

Joined Up Business Networking www.joinedupnetworking.com

Referral generation groups

Athena http://theathenanetwork.co.uk

BNI www.bni.com

4Networking www.4networking.biz

Women in Business Network www.wibn.co.uk

Organisations that run regular networking events

Local Chambers of Commerce

Institute of Directors www.iod.com

Professional associations

Federation of Small Businesses www.fsb.org.uk

Parent-friendly networking groups

Mum's Business Club www.mumsbusinessclub.com

Mum's the boss www.mumstheboss.co.uk

Communal working groups

Jelly groups www.workatjelly.com

5

Online networking options

What topics are covered in this chapter?

- The types of informal and formal online networking
- What we mean by a social networking site and a micro-blogging site
- How to generate referrals using online networking
- How to maximise your effectiveness whilst networking online

In the previous chapter we looked at all the different face-to-face networking options available to today's professionals. All of these options require the networker to be present physically with another person. What happens when you have the motivation to network, but not the opportunity or time to go out and meet people? Or what happens if your target market does not reside locally to you? This is where online networking has the advantage over face-to-face networking.

Online networking lets you network all day and night, regardless of where you are in the world and who you are with. All you need is an internet connection or 3G/4G signal – you don't even need someone else online at the time to network.

There are many different forms of online networking:

- Twitter
- social networking sites, e.g. LinkedIn, Facebook, Google+
- online forums.

Similar to face-to-face networking, these different types of online networking help you do one or more of the following things:

■ improve your profile, i.e. being 'found'

■ generate opportunities, such as a new job or new clients

■ extend and strengthen the community around you

■ find solutions.

There are literally millions of social networking sites and online forums on the internet. Each site and forum will have its own focus, community, culture and social etiquette. In this chapter I will be talking about the most widely available sites that will have the most impact on your networking activities. I was talking recently with the ex-managing director of LinkedIn and asked him which social networking sites were going to be the important ones over the next five years. His opinion was LinkedIn (of course!), Twitter, Facebook and specialist social networking sites, such as AccountingWeb, which cater to niche audiences. Therefore, in this chapter I will be focusing on these three social networking sites, and Google+. At this point in time, May 2014, the jury is still out on whether Google+ will make it as a mainstream social networking site.

In fact, the combination of LinkedIn, Twitter, Facebook and Google+ with a blog, is what will deliver a huge impact to your networking activities, and should be your focus when you start online networking. In the next chapter we will look at how to use a blog as a business networking tool.

Generating referrals using online networking

Unlike BNI groups, there is no such direct equivalent of a referral marketing organisation in the online networking world. By this I mean no large formal or commercial platforms or communities where groups of like-minded individuals from different professions get together to generate referrals for each other. However, the opportunity score equation, as I have proved within my own businesses (see Chapter 2), still works for online networking – i.e. the more time you invest in demonstrating your credibility, helping others, building a consistent and marketable personal brand and being visible to your target market, the more likelihood there is that opportunities will come your way via your online network.

Make it consistent

❝Trust takes longer to build up and is quicker to destroy❞

Consistency, just like integrity and reliability, is very important in the virtual world, as it forms the basis of trust in an online relationship. Trust takes longer to build up and is quicker to destroy within the virtual world. Make sure the messages on your website, Twitter biography, Facebook page, LinkedIn, Google+ and other online sites where you maintain a profile are all consistent. For example, you should use the same avatar for each online profile.

What is a 'social networking' site?

'Social media is collections of data and information, whereas social networking is collections of people.'

Peter Rees, E-marketing Systems[1]

A social networking site is a type of 'social media' – however, the terms social media and social networking are wrongly used interchangeably. A social networking site exists to connect people together to form an online community.

A social networking site tends to include the following pieces of functionality:

■ user profiles

■ a way to connect between users, e.g. Facebook 'friends', LinkedIn 'connections', Twitter 'followers', Google+ circles

■ forums where users can post up and join in discussions

■ a place for users to blog

■ articles – normally written by the users

■ groups or communities of users – for example, the LinkedIn and Facebook groups, Google+ communities

■ private or open messaging between users

■ SMS online chat between site users

■ a status update or facility to share your thoughts with all the site's users.

For example, UK Business Forums (www.ukbusinessforums.co.uk) is one of the UK's biggest forums for entrepreneurs and business owners. Although it is a social networking site, it is best known for its busy and vibrant forums.

---

[1] http://wsiebusiness.co.uk/blog/

For a list of major social networking sites and online forums, please see 'Further resources' at the end of the book.

LinkedIn

What is LinkedIn?

> **Tip**
>
> If you use only one social networking site or social media tool, then choose LinkedIn.

LinkedIn is a social networking site and has been described as 'Facebook for professionals'. In June 2013 it reported that it had 225 million professions in more than 200 countries. When I wrote the first edition of this book, back in the autumn of 2010, LinkedIn had only 75 million users. As LinkedIn has always steadily grown its user numbers *and* been profitable, I strongly suspect that this growth will continue for some time. If Twitter is the online networking equivalent of being in the world's largest bar, and Facebook is where you relax after a hard day at work, LinkedIn is where you go when you are at work. In other words, LinkedIn's culture is very professional and, to use LinkedIn effectively, your updates, questions and presence need to be professionally, rather than personally, orientated.

LinkedIn can be used as a contact book, CV, references book and a place where you can learn from your peers and connect with potential clients. Probably the best way to think about LinkedIn is as your online professional shop window where, literally, you showcase your professional credibility.

What are the benefits of using LinkedIn?

LinkedIn enables you to establish a professional profile on the web. If you Google your name, your LinkedIn profile normally will be returned in the first page and, unless you have a heavy online presence, within the top three results in Google. This means that your LinkedIn profile is likely to be the first place where someone checks out your online identity, i.e. the all-important 'first impression'. LinkedIn enables you to control this 'first impression'. More importantly, if you meet someone or are recommended to someone, there is a very strong possibility that they will check out your credibility on LinkedIn. If you are not on LinkedIn or have a poorly completed LinkedIn profile, this may stop them developing the relationship,

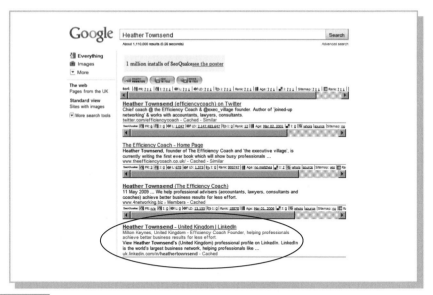

figure 5.1   Google your name to find your LinkedIn profile

conversation about a possible vacancy or potential piece of business any further.

LinkedIn is a great way of extending your reach and network. When you are connected to people, normally you can view their connections. This allows you to use LinkedIn proactively to ask for introductions to people that your network knows, i.e. the face-to-face equivalent of being able to look through someone's little black book of contacts. As well as viewing people's connections, LinkedIn allows you to search its database for users and organisations. This is a great tool if you want to build up a prospects list or help fill in any gaps in your network map (see Chapter 13). This ability to extend your reach on LinkedIn and see your network's network is great if you are looking for a new job or new business opportunities.

LinkedIn is one of the places where headhunters and recruiters, looking for professionals, search for candidates. Either they will use LinkedIn to supplement their own candidate database, or LinkedIn has become their candidate database. I was contacted by a recruiter who had searched for 'leadership' + 'learning and development' on LinkedIn, and I had turned up in his search (See Figure 5.1).

'We have gone from job searching to people searching.'

Dan Schawbel, *author of* Me 2.0: Build a powerful brand to achieve career success

> **❝LinkedIn allows you to establish a strong personal brand❞**

In today's fast-changing world, people move jobs and locations constantly. After you have left an organisation it can be difficult to maintain contact with the network from your old organisation. Once you are on LinkedIn and connected with others, you remain connected to them, even when they change their job and move to the other side of the world.

LinkedIn allows you to start up groups, as well as join groups. Each group membership is based around a particular theme or purpose. The communities within these groups are great places to ask questions, demonstrate your credibility and find help. There are two different types of groups on LinkedIn, open and closed groups. Open groups allow anyone to see what is being discussed in the group, whereas only members of closed groups can see the discussions. The best-performing groups, i.e. the most vibrant and engaged communities, tend to be very heavily moderated. Therefore, do find out the group rules before posting or contributing within a group.

LinkedIn allows you to establish a strong personal brand, by giving you the ability to write about yourself in the summary and experience sections, as well as embedding rich media, i.e. videos, documents, presentations within your LinkedIn profile. You can strengthen your personal brand by sharing key pieces of valuable content with your audience via your profile. This content could be:

- a short video clip of you introducing yourself and what you do
- PR clippings, such as when you have been quoted in a press article
- a brochure about your organisation
- an article that helps your audience solve some of its problems
- a presentation that you gave at a recent conference on an industry 'hot topic'.

Companies and organisations also have a presence on LinkedIn. Similar to Twitter, LinkedIn members can now 'follow' a company. This allows them to see company news or when someone has been promoted, been hired or left. If you are interested in working for or with an organisation, this functionality enables you to target the organisation effectively – or even anticipate a vacancy that will be of interest to you. Use the company page to see how you are connected to employees of the company. Then use your network to get introductions to the people in the company with whom you want to build a relationship.

> **Tip**
>
> Use the LinkedIn company page feature to help you build stronger and deeper relationships within your customer and client organisations.

How to maximise your effectiveness on LinkedIn

Like any social networking medium you need to decide first why and how you will use LinkedIn to advance your career or business. For example, if you decide you want to change your current role, you need to have decided on what role you are looking for. It is no good branding your LinkedIn profile for a role within a professional practice, if you decide you want to go in-house. Bryony Thomas, author of *Watertight Marketing*, uses LinkedIn to maintain relationships with people, clients and suppliers she has worked with and would recommend to others.

Your LinkedIn profile is your shop window to the world. You need to make sure your profile is displaying the 'goods', i.e. your brand, that you want potential clients or recruiters to buy from you. Far too many people treat their LinkedIn profile as their online CV, and very often a poorly completed online CV! You are more likely to be found and contacted on LinkedIn if you fill out your profile fully. As well as fully completing your LinkedIn profile, you want to make sure that it supports the brand you want to portray. For example:

- Change the professional headline from the default 'job role at company' to something that describes more meaningfully who you are and what you do. To help you get found in a LinkedIn search, make sure you use keywords in your professional headline that your target audience will be searching for.

- Use the summary section to showcase some examples of what you do, how you do it and the typical results you get.

- Avoid lots of 'corporatese' or marketing-type words in your profile, and make sure your profile is 'easy on the eye' and inviting.

- Use the experience and projects section to give fuller details of your responsibilities in each role or major project.

- Change around the order of your recommendations so that your most powerful ones appear in the top two places. This will make sure they are more likely to been seen by anyone reading your profile.

∎ Fill out your profile in the first, rather than third, person. The thinking behind this is that the first person can make you seem more personable and approachable.

∎ Commit to your personal brand in your profile, rather than trying to brand yourself as all things to all people. For example, despite what some people claim, you can't *specialise* in small and medium-sized enterprises (SMEs), professional practices, social enterprises *and* not-for-profits.

Many professionals are reluctant to add in any personal information to their LinkedIn profile. Whilst you do want to focus 80–90 per cent of your LinkedIn profile on the professional part of your life, you do want to leave in some personal details or what I call 'relationship hooks'. People still want to buy people – and if they get a truer sense of who you are and your personality via your LinkedIn profile, they are more likely to choose to make a connection with you. Your use of 'relationship hooks' allows them to start a conversation with you. For example, on my LinkedIn profile I use a relationship hook when I talk about accidentally becoming a writer. How many of you now want to ask me how I accidentally became a writer?

The more content on your profile that enhances your credibility and personal brand – e.g. recommendations, presentations and documents on your specialist subjects – the more opportunities are likely to come your way.

Tip

Next time you meet up with a contact, take the time to look through their LinkedIn connections. Pick one of two people from their connections list and ask your contact for an introduction.

LinkedIn can be your very own micro-PR machine. Regularly tell potential employers, clients and recruiters what you have achieved or are doing in the course of your normal working life. For example, via the status update function, tell people about great client wins, new recommendations, product or service launches and networking meetings you are attending.

Tip

Regularly, ideally daily, check to see who has looked at your LinkedIn profile. Eighty per cent of the time it is because someone is being nosey. The remaining 20 per cent of the time is probably because either they are thinking of you for something or maybe they want to use your services or hire you for a role. Do get in contact with people who have viewed your profile to find out why.

To attract opportunities via LinkedIn, you need to be a real person, not just a name in someone's contact list. Far too many people on LinkedIn indulge in what I call *contact collection*. It doesn't matter how many connections you have on LinkedIn if,

■ you don't actively use LinkedIn

■ you don't try to develop the connections you have on LinkedIn into a real life relationship

■ your connections on LinkedIn are not well-placed to help you achieve your networking goals.

As relationships, trust and credibility develop more quickly in the real, rather than the virtual, world, always aim to take the important relationships out of LinkedIn and into the real world.

A daily routine for LinkedIn

The best way to use LinkedIn is to go into it daily, and allocate 10 minutes to it. In your 10 minutes complete the following:

■ Check your notifications to see whether there is any conversation or activity to which you need to respond.

■ See who has looked at your LinkedIn profile and start a conversation or connect with anyone who potentially is useful to you.

■ Add something to your status update that is useful to your network on LinkedIn, such as an article, or a piece of personal PR.

■ Look down your LinkedIn wall and interact with one person in your LinkedIn network.

■ Contribute one thing to one group on LinkedIn.

Twitter

What is Twitter?

Many people have dismissed Twitter as just boring, trivial chat. Who wants to know what you ate for lunch? Who cares what the latest 'in' celebrity has just tweeted? It is true that much of the conversation on Twitter is fairly mundane. However, if you were at a mix-and-mingle networking event, I'm guessing that most of your conversation that evening would be fairly mundane and classed as trivial chit-chat.

Twitter is a micro-blogging site. Users of the service post short messages, called 'tweets', of up to 140 characters in length. Users choose to follow people or lists of people. Following means that you see all of their updates, or 'tweets'.

Within Twitter you can privately message another person or 'peep', as long as they follow you, and you can send an open message or reply to any other users, as long as you know their Twitter name. Unless you choose to protect your tweets, so that only people you have approved can see them, everyone can see everyone else's tweets.

What are the benefits of using Twitter?

Twitter gives you an instant international reach and visibility. Unless you have protected your tweets, i.e. they will not show up in the public time-line, your tweets can be seen by anyone, anywhere, at any time. At the time of writing I have more than 11,000 followers, who are spread all over the world, but mostly within the UK. Every time I tweet there is a possibility that 11,000 people who follow me will see that tweet. Be warned, though, that if you say something stupid or insulting on Twitter, a lot of people may see it and spread it, before you can erase it.

> **Twitter gives you an instant international reach and visibility**

The visibility and accessibility of Twitter means it is a great tool to drive traffic to your website. When I started the Joined Up Business Networking blog (www.joinedupnetworking.com), I needed to generate traffic quickly to the blog – and did not want to wait for the search engine optimisation to kick in, or to pay for web traffic. By writing and publishing a blog post every day, and tweeting once about the new blog post, I generated 1,000 visitors to the website in the first month it was up.

Twitter is sometimes referred to as an open networking tool: everyone can contact everyone else, regardless of status or prior relationships. If you are enjoying reading this book, how about sending me a tweet? I'm @ HeatherTowns on Twitter.[2] It's this accessibility that enables you to find and connect quickly and effectively with your target market. For example, when I started on Twitter, I deliberately began to follow accountants and lawyers. This was how I found and 'met' Chris Sherliker, managing partner of Silverman Sherliker LLP.[3] Six months later, Chris became one of my first clients sourced from Twitter.

Hashtags or words with a # put in front of them, are used to denote a keyword on Twitter. They are often used to help people on Twitter join in with relevant conversations. For example, attendees at the CIPD Coaching

[2] www.twitter.com/HeatherTowns and www.twitter.com/joinedupnetwork
[3] www.twitter.com/london_law_firm

Conference 2013 event were asked to tweet during the event using the event hashtag, #CIPDcoaching13. Other attendees and non-attendees can then search on the event hashtag to join in the conversation, but also 'meet' other people with similar personal or professional interests. Television or radio programmes often will have a hashtag to enable people watching the programme to talk to each other on Twitter.

How to maximise your effectiveness on Twitter

Unlike LinkedIn, where the site's etiquette expects professional rather than personal updates, to use Twitter effectively you need to be the 'whole' person. What do I mean by the whole person? If you were networking at a large mix-and-mingle type of event, you would be bored rapidly by anyone who talked only work, didn't disclose their personal side or didn't listen to what you had to say. It's the same with Twitter. People want to get to know you as a real person, and you will be more effective on Twitter if you talk about both the personal and professional parts of your life, and engage with people. This means that you need to fill out your bio and include a good, professional-looking picture within your profile.

> **Tip**
>
> Within your bio include keywords containing your target market, e.g. 'I work with accountants and lawyers'.

'To succeed on Twitter you need to show your whole personality and engage as an individual.'

Brian Inkster, Inksters Solicitors[4]

Very easily Twitter can be used ineffectively as a networking tool. Before you start tweeting, it is essential that you know what you are trying to achieve by being on Twitter. For example, if you want to build relationships with people within your target market, you need to be looking actively to follow and engage with your target market on Twitter.

> **Tip**
>
> To use Twitter to build up your personal brand and credibility, regularly tweet out links to articles on your blog.

---

[4] www.twitter.com/brianinkster

It's very easy to get seduced into trying to build up a follower base fast. It's not the number of followers you have that counts; it's the number of engaged followers you have.

To find out how engaged someone's follower base is, take a look at the number of lists that they have been included on. The higher the number of lists someone is included on, the greater the level of engagement within their follower base.

The challenge of using Twitter effectively is to minimise the noise – i.e. the tweets of people who either are not relevant to you, or say things that are not relevant right now. This is where lists and hashtags come in. In Twitter, set up lists of people who are really important to you, for example, your clients, personal friends and family, introducers, potential employers, prospects, journalists, etc. Then check these lists every day and interact with the people with whom you need to maintain a high level of visibility.

Most journalists, from the trade, local and national press, hang out on Twitter. Whilst they may not be tweeting actively, they will always be listening out for potential stories and experts to help them with their own stories. Very often, if they want help with a story, a journalist will add a #journorequest to their tweets.

Twitter is a very quick and fast-paced environment. Frequently news will break on Twitter faster than over the TV and newspaper networks. In fact, now you see newspapers 'breaking' stories that first appeared on Twitter and become the story on Twitter! To get the most out of Twitter you do need to commit to use it daily.

Remember that, just as you are trying to find and interact with people on Twitter, so are other people. Therefore, make it as easy as possible for others to interact with you on Twitter by:

- tweeting something at least a couple of times a day
- asking questions on your tweets – you never know who may answer them!
- including some 'small talk tweets', such as 'looking forward to a lovely lunch with a friend, what are you up to today?'
- mixing up your content, not just tweeting links to a blog or retweeting others' content.

---

case study   It all started with a tweet

When I started writing the first edition of the *FT Guide*, I put out a tweet asking for reviewers for the book. Robert Watson (@drdrdr09), a business coach from Australia, answered my tweet. He then went on to professionally edit the first edition of the book for free. Yes, seriously. This act of giving, or 'paying forward', then led to him changing career and becoming a highly regarded and sought-after book editor. Since this point he has gone on to edit at least eight more published books and countless self-published books.

Facebook

What is Facebook?

Facebook is currently the biggest social networking site, with, at the time of writing, more than 1.1 billion users. In 2010 it had 500 million active users. This is equivalent to one in every seven people in the world using Facebook. Facebook users can add people as friends and send them messages, and update their personal profiles to notify friends about themselves. Facebook is a site rich with functionality, and users can post videos, links, updates – even play online games with their friends.

> **Facebook is a place where you can contact your personal network quickly**

Although Facebook is a purely 'social' network – this is where people let their hair down at the end of the day – it does have a place in the professional's business networking toolkit. For example, if you are using your personal and professional network to job hunt, Facebook is a place where you can contact your personal network quickly. Look through any user's 'friends' and normally you will see a high proportion of people they are currently working with, or have worked with in the past.

Many firms and businesses see Facebook as a distraction from work and sometimes will block employees' access to Facebook on company systems. However, in the past couple of years, Facebook has evolved into a true business tool, so I expect that we will see more businesses opening up access to Facebook to their employees. Plus, mobile phone technology is now such that most people can access Facebook via their smartphone rather than relying on their company's IT systems.

What are the benefits of using Facebook?

Facebook is huge. Any adult between the age of 18 and 55 who is not on Facebook is now in the minority. Connecting with someone on Facebook is rapidly becoming the preferred mechanism for staying in touch with someone you like.

Facebook allows you to have business pages as well as a personal account. Many businesses and special interest groups, particularly sports clubs and small professional service firms, are using Facebook groups as a way of actively keeping in touch and engaging with their members and clients.

How to maximise your effectiveness on Facebook

To get the most out of Facebook, you need to decide how you want to use it. It's absolutely fine to use Facebook just for purely social reasons – and that's all many professionals use it for.

Facebook is a different communication medium to LinkedIn or Twitter. What works on LinkedIn and Twitter won't always work on Facebook. For example, on Facebook people tend to update their status once or maybe twice a day. If you are a regular tweeter and tweet 10 or more times a day and decide to display your tweets via Facebook, it's a quick way to annoy your connections.

Tip

If you want to use Facebook as a business development tool, then use a business page to do this. Your personal network on Facebook will become fed up rapidly with reading your marketing updates on their Facebook stream.

To promote engagement with the people who 'like' your business page, remember to update the status once or twice a day, and keep the updates very chatty and personable. People want to be entertained on Facebook rather than 'sold' to. The types of post that tend to engage with your Facebook fans include:

- visuals with added quotes or messages
- funny cartoons or short video clips
- personal updates
- motivational quotes.

Google+

What is Google+?

Google+ is Google's third attempt at building a social network to rival Facebook and LinkedIn. The jury is out as to whether this attempt will be successful. Technically, Google+ is the second largest social network, as it has over 500 million users. However, according to research by +Gigya in July 2013, it was only responsible for 2 per cent of all social sharing. Contrast this with 50 per cent of all social sharing happening via Facebook.

The main difference between Facebook, LinkedIn, Twitter and Google+ is that you use 'circles' to organise your Google+ connections. Then you can share information with different circles rather than with all your followers.

What are the benefits of using Google+?

Probably the biggest benefit of being on Google+ is its deep integration with Google's search engine. When you share a link on Google+ it becomes instantly indexed by the search engine, rather than having to wait until a 'Google spider' has found the page on your website. The more you interact on Google+ and share your posts and content, the more importance Google will attach to your links and blogs. This will help your websites and content rise up the Google search engine ranking.

Unlike the very restrictive limits on what you can share on Twitter, you can share pretty much anything on Google+. This means that, if you so wish, you can use Google+ as a blogging platform. This is something that you can't do very easily on Facebook or LinkedIn.

Google is in the process of aiming to integrate many of its products, tools and systems with Google+. So where, previously, you could register on Google places and show up in local search results, now you have to have a verified Google+ business page to get listed in Google+ Local. The businesses in Google+ Local are the ones featured now when local search results appear in the search engine results.

Google+ communities are a great way of sharing information and conversations with like-minded people in open communities or small private groups, such as your team, in private communities. The Google+ communities are Google's way of replicating forums, LinkedIn groups or Facebook groups.

One of the best features of Google+ is the ability to host video conference calls with your Google+ network via the hangouts. A hangout is, basically, the Google+ name for a video conference call. These can be recorded and reused as marketing material for your business.

How to maximise your effectiveness on Google+

The challenge faced by many Google+ users, particularly very heavy users of Facebook, LinkedIn or Twitter, is finding the time to invest in yet another social networking site. Therefore, aim to adopt a routine where you go into Google+ daily and do one of the following things:

- Find someone new to follow and add into a circle.
- Go into a relevant Google+ community and post up a reply or a '+1' to a discussion.
- Post up a discussion on your Google+ page, and share a link to a blog post in the discussion.

Whilst, at the time of writing, the engagement on Google+ is very low compared to the other big social networks, this may change!

Online forums

What are online forums?

These are websites where registered users can post discussions or contribute to discussions by replying to the original post. Most online forums are part of a bigger social networking site. For example, a Facebook business page or private Ning network comes with its own online forum integrated. In fact, many social networking sites, e.g. UK Business Forums (www.ukbusinessforums.co.uk), are better known as an online forum rather than a social networking site.

What are the benefits of using online forums?

Online forums are a great way to connect and demonstrate your credibility with your target audience. Most industry sectors and special interest groups have a forum somewhere dedicated to them and their particular requirements.

Online forums are a great way to find answers. I regularly use AccountingWeb, the largest online community of accountants, to engage with my target audience.

How to maximise your effectiveness with online forums

You will achieve work and referrals via business forums only if you are pre-pared to be helpful and share your specialist knowledge. When answering a question on a forum, remember to read the question properly and answer the question (and subsequent questions asked in the threads). Building up a consistent track record for sharing your knowledge helps you build trust and credibility with the forum's users.

> **❝You are aiming to interact with people and build up a relationship❞**

Trust and credibility are vital for you to gain work via the connections you have made on an online business forum. Everyone is aware that an online connection may not be who they say they are. Often this is the reason that it takes longer to develop relationships, and ultimately business, via your online, rather than offline, networking. You gain credibility and trust if you are connected to your online contacts on more than one online forum or platform.

Remember that when you are on an internet forum, you are aiming to interact with people and build up a relationship. By freely offering your contact details, you will be surprised how many people do contact you directly. A relationship normally develops more quickly if you take it offline, e.g. a phone call or face-to-face meeting.

Business-orientated internet forums are not the place to sell. I'm serious. Don't sell. When you are out networking, how much do you hate being sold to? It's the same on forums. Forum users can spot this a mile off. Posts like this (with no helpful information)...

'I've got loads of experience with your problem, give me a call on xxxx xxxxx, and I will talk you through it'

...are selling, and tend to infuriate people rather than showcase your exper-tise and credibility.

Many forums will let you put a standard email signature onto the bottom of all your posts, plus include links in your general text. This is fantastic for search engine optimisation. What keywords are important to you? How can you incorporate these keywords into a phrase that will entice people to click onto the link through to your website? For example, instead of hyper-linking 'JS Accounting Services' back to your website, what about 'find out how to save up to 20 per cent off your accountancy bills'.

Different groups of people frequent different forums. To maximise your effectiveness on forums you need to make sure you are in a forum with people you would like to meet. For example, if you want to meet female entrepreneurs, work-at-home mums or start-up businesses (run by females), then you want to hang around in the everywoman site (www.everywoman. com). If you want to meet business owners with a significant overseas membership, then UK Business Forums (www.ukbusinessforums.co.uk) is a good place to hang out.

Each forum attracts different types of people and each site will have its own way of doing things. I maintain a heavy presence on three different business forums and they are like chalk and cheese. Two of these sites are heavily moderated and any selling or misuse of the forum is quickly curtailed. The other site is more tolerant of some light advertising by members.

To help you achieve an effective level of visibility on a forum, turn on the daily digest facility. This facility enables you to monitor conversations rather than having to go into the forums and 'hunt' for new conversations.

Summary

There are millions of online networking sites, but serious business networkers need to maintain a presence on LinkedIn, Twitter, Facebook and Google+. These four sites will generate profile, i.e. visibility, for you.

The etiquette of each social networking site is different. Savvy networkers take the time to understand the subtleties of each site and how to use it effectively.

You need only an internet connection to network online. As trust takes longer to build using purely online networking, aim to take the relationship offline to generate a stronger, deeper relationship more quickly.

When networking online, make sure you take the time to 'engage' with the people you are connecting and tweeting with.

ACTION POINTS

■ Join LinkedIn, Twitter, Google+ and Facebook.

■ Write a short and a long bio about you for your online profiles. A short bio normally is limited to fewer than 200 characters.

■ Find a decent professional head-and-shoulders shot of yourself to use in your online profiles.

■ Find out on which sites your target market hangs out online. Register for these sites and set yourself a goal of visiting them daily and posting something on the site every day.

■ Fully complete your LinkedIn profile and brand it for the job you want rather than the job you have now.

Further resources

Books

Brogan, C., *Social Media 101: Tactics and tips to develop your business online*, John Wiley & Sons, 2010.

Halligan, B. and Shah, D., *Inbound Marketing: Get found using Google, social media and blogs*, John Wiley & Sons, 2009.

Kawasaki, G., *What the Plus! Google+ for the rest of us*, McGraw-Hill Professional, 2012.

Qualman, E., *Socialnomics: How social media transforms the way we live and do business*, John Wiley & Sons, 2nd edn, 2012.

Schawbel, D., *Me 2.0: Build a powerful brand to achieve career success*, Kaplan Trade, revised edn, 2010.

Websites and blogs

Chris Brogan's blog www.chrisbrogan.com

Just Professionals www.justprofessionals.net

LinkedIn and Twitter training www.joinedupnetworking.com

Mashable http://mashable.com

Social networking sites

For a list of major social networking sites, see 'Further resources' at the end of the book.

6

Blogging

What topics are covered in this chapter?

- ■ What is blogging?
- ■ How to use blogging to enhance your credibility and personal brand

In the last chapter, we discussed the four main online networking sites, LinkedIn, Twitter, Google+ and Facebook. These sites give you profile and visibility, but the impact of these sites is significantly heightened when used in conjunction with a well-written blog. It's the blog which gives you credibility and communicates your online personal brand to your audience. When you combine an active presence in online networking sites with a well-written blog, you are generating all four of the ingredients, as discussed in Chapter 2, needed for networking success: credibility, personal brand, visibility and social capital. In this chapter we show you how to use a blog as a networking tool and how to use it effectively in conjunction with your online networking activity.

What is blogging?

A blog is a form of website where you can self-publish articles without needing the approval of anyone else. The prospect of being able to publish anything and everything may be very appealing to you; however, as a net-worker, your aim is to write intelligent and thought-provoking pieces that establish your credibility as an expert in your specialist subject, and invite people to interact with you on your blog.

❝Your aim is to write intelligent and thought-provoking pieces❞

A blog post is not like a magazine article or feature. The ideal length of a blog post is 200–500 words, i.e. long enough to give you something of value, but short enough to be digested in 5–10 minutes.

Unlike traditional printed newspapers and magazines, anyone can start a blog in minutes. There are many free blogging tools, e.g. WordPress (www.wordpress.com) and Blogger (www.blogger.com), which will allow you to set up a free account and start blogging.

A blogger, i.e. the individual who maintains the blog, regularly updates the content on the site with short articles, i.e. blog posts. Most blogs are interactive, allowing visitors to comment. Blogs can be anything from an online magazine with hundreds of thousands of regular readers, such as Mashable (http://mashable.com), to an individual's online diary and personal journal, which a few select friends and family are allowed to access.

It is this interactivity that enables blogging to be used as a networking tool. Chris Sherliker, managing partner of Silverman Sherliker LLP, maintains a blog – www.silvermansherlikerblog.com – and blogged about the pressures of legal practice in November 2009.[1] This was a subject near and dear to my own heart, and I left a lengthy comment about the impact of the chargeable time culture on the legal profession. This comment, and subsequent discussion later, led to me being invited to work with the firm extensively in 2010.

The point of a blog is to help people see past the commercial literature and help connect with you as a person, i.e. your personal brand – which is vital if you are to generate opportunities via your blogging activities. Your blog is a great tool to build up trust and credibility with your target audience, showing them you understand them, and know what you are talking about. In the world of online networking, your blog is your main asset to demonstrate your credibility with your target audience and strengthen your online personal brand.

What are the benefits of blogging?

A blog is a fantastic destination point to showcase your credibility to your target audience. When your target market 'meets' you in the online world, often they are interested to know whether you are the real deal or not. A

---

[1] www.silvermansherlikerblog.com/developing-ninja-lawyer-skills

well-maintained blog, which you direct people to read, either via Twitter or a link on a forum post, is the easiest way to build up your credibility and strengthen your online personal brand.

Your page rank in Google is influenced heavily by how much fresh content you have on your website. As a blog is dynamic, i.e. users can interact with the website, Google is more likely to place a greater weight on a blog rather than a static website. This means that maintaining a keyword-rich blog is vital for effective search engine optimisation. Owning a website that features highly in the search engine rankings is a way of generating a ready-made interested audience to interact with, i.e. to network with you.

Your blog posts can be used to keep in touch with your network. For example, tweeting links to them, adding them to your LinkedIn status update, starting a discussion on Google+ or sending them to your network via email is a great way of increasing your visibility whilst strengthening your credibility. For example, I frequently find potential new clients getting in touch with me solely because they regularly follow the links I place on my LinkedIn status update to my blog posts.

Most people now, when they have a problem or question, go to the internet to find the answers. Whilst at this point they may not be ready to buy, if it is your blog post that helps educate them, they are far more likely to come back to you when they do need your services. Consequently, a blog is a great way to educate your network, not only in what you do, the results you get and who you do it for, but also why they may need your services in the future.

How to maximise your effectiveness with blogging

Similar to any kind of networking, to blog effectively you need to clarify why you are starting a blog and who you are writing it for. A well-written and thought-out blog will be a great source of credibility and strengthens your personal brand. A badly thought-out or written blog will be a drain on your time, reduce the impact of your personal brand, and damage your credibility.

Think about your target client. What sort of things will interest them? What problems or challenges do they face in their everyday lives? What do they read? What websites do they spend time surfing on?

Make sure you are always writing about subjects that are of value to your target audience, as this will encourage them to read, comment on and return to your blog. Keeping a blog regularly updated takes time and effort, which is fine when you are light on client work. However, there will be times when you have some major client deadlines to meet and no spare time to blog. Your blog doesn't always need to be written by you. (I've often used guest blogs to help keep my blog updated when I am low on time.) Who else within your firm, team, department or network writes well and would be happy to write for your blog? In fact, I, personally, write a few of my clients' blogs for them. They don't like writing and I do – it is a win-win situation!

> ### Tip
>
> Whenever you read a blog post that would be of value to your target audience, ask the blogger if you can republish it on your site, with full author credits. Unless they are a direct competitor of yours, most bloggers will say 'Yes' and be genuinely flattered!

Using blogging as an effective networking tool is more than you solely pumping out content. The point of blogging as a networking tool is to connect with other people and to encourage people to read your blog. If you spend time commenting on other people's blogs, they will look at your blog and start to engage with your content. They may even ask you for a guest blog.

❝They may even ask you for a guest blog❞

An effective blog is visible to your target market. This means writing regular, fresh content and encouraging people within your online network to read your new content. Here are some suggestions of how to encourage people to read your blog:

- Post links on Twitter, your LinkedIn status update, Facebook and Google+ to newly written blog posts.
- Create a discussion on LinkedIn or other online networking sites and use your blog post within the discussion.
- Include a link to a blog post when you are answering a question in an online forum.
- Add a link to your blog in your email signature or forum signature.

Ten questions to help you improve the effectiveness of your blog

1 How will this post interest my target audience?
2 How will this post add value to my target audience?
3 Have I got a beginning, middle and end to my post?
4 Am I posting frequently enough for my target audience?
5 Is my post too long for the attention span of my target audience?
6 Is my blog post unique, i.e. not duplicated elsewhere on the web (to improve the search engine ranking for the blog post)?
7 Am I putting important keywords into my post (to help the blog post get found)?
8 Does this post sound like me? (Or does my ghost blogger sound like me?)
9 How does this post link to my objectives for my blog?
10 Can I add a question to the end of my blog to encourage comments?

Many people ask the question, 'How often should I blog?' The right answer is based on how often your target audience expects to read your blog. For example, some bloggers blog a couple of times a day, but post up short sharp posts, and other bloggers write in-depth articles weekly. The right frequency will be based on the length, depth and breadth of your content, and what your target audience expects. If you don't know what will work with your target audience, experiment with writing different length articles, and how often you blog. Typically, I recommend to my clients that they aim to write at a frequency they know they can maintain in the long term. Writing regularly, once a fortnight, is far better than trying to write a couple of times a week and leaving big gaps in your blog when you don't manage this.

Eighteen ideas for what you can blog about

1 Book reviews.
2 Presentations you have prepared.
3 Proposals you have prepared.
4 Video clips of you presenting at a seminar or conference.
5 Lists of great websites or books that you think people should read.
6 Anything that highlights your personal credentials.
7 Any training events that you attend.
8 Anything that occurs to you that may be of interest to your target audience.

9 New products or services that you are starting to sell.

10 Introductions to new team members.

11 Case studies.

12 Testimonials received from happy clients.

13 Achievements of happy clients.

14 What a client or you learned whilst working together.

15 Interviews with experts inside and outside of your firm.

16 Responses to news items or articles.

17 Thought for the day.

18 How-to articles.

What do you need to include on your blog?

It's your blog so, unless you maintain it on behalf of your employers, you have total editorial freedom. However, this is what we recommend, as a minimum, you include on your blog:

- Contact details – how can people get in contact with you? Include both a telephone number and email address, as different people prefer different ways of getting in touch.

- A page about you – include a professional-looking photograph and biography.

- A call to action – what do you want them to do as a result of reading your blog? Sign up for your mailing list?

- Links to your presence on social networking sites, e.g. Twitter, LinkedIn, Google+ and Facebook.

- Links to your company's website.

The importance of your blog post's title

People will take a decision to click through and read your blog post, based on its title. This means that the title of your blog post is more important than the actual content. To influence a person to click through and actually read your blog post, a title needs to either promise value to the reader or pique their curiosity. A compelling title will help your article get noticed by an editor or guest blogger, who may request to use your content on their site.

Titles that help your blog post get more 'clicks' normally fall into the following categories:

■ Clearly states what the post will deliver in the title, e.g. 'Six tips to avoid stirring up trouble on social media'.

■ Promises to help people save money or time, e.g. 'Simple ways all business owners can legally minimise their tax bill'.

■ Has a counter-intuitive title, e.g. I once put this headline on my local branch's Chartered Institute of Personnel and Development (CIPD) newsletter: 'Why you shouldn't renew your CIPD membership'.

■ 'Scares' your target market, e.g. 'Are you *legally* signing people up to your mailing list?'

■ Includes your target audience's name in the title, e.g. 'Money laundering – what every business owner needs to know to keep themselves safe and legal'.

How to use a blog post to win business

I often hear people saying, 'I have a blog but I don't know how to use it to win business.' Here are some ideas that my clients and my network and I have used to win business from our blogs.

Write about subjects that your clients want answers to

The more helpful you can be to the readership of your blog, the more likely they will get in touch with you. Many professionals worry about giving away too much intellectual property on their blog. Ultimately, this isn't normally possible as most of the information is already on the web, you've just got to look hard enough.

Blog about client case studies

Whilst you do want to keep a good balance between valuable content for your clients and self-serving blog posts, blogging about successful client case studies can help to generate new clients. These case studies, if converted into a useful blog post for readers of your blog, can help them personally, whilst showing what you can do for your clients. This type of blog post is great to circulate around your network, particularly to anyone who is in a position to introduce you.

Blog about subjects that motivate your clients to take action

Many professionals find that their biggest competitor is not down the road but a potential client's inherent inertia to take action. Using blog posts, which demonstrate the risk of doing nothing and why it pays to take action now, can help convert a potential client into a real client.

RSS feeds and feed readers

'RSS allows me to read all my favourite stuff in one place.'
Su Butcher, social media expert to the construction industry

> **Tip**
>
> Sign up to Google Feedburner to get statistics of who has subscribed to your RSS feed, as well as offer your blog readers the opportunity to get your new blog posts automatically emailed to them.

RSS, which stands for Really Simple Syndication, is a way of reading frequently updated web pages, such as blogs or news websites, for example www.bbc.co.uk. An RSS feed reader – such as Feedly – is a piece of software that allows you to access all your RSS feeds in one place.

Whenever you see the RSS icon (see Figure 6.1) this means that the website has the facility for you to add its feed to the feed reader of your choice.

figure 6.1   The RSS icon

For example, if you have three or four blogs that you like to read, you can add their RSS feed to your RSS feed reader and, whenever a new blog post is published, it will be placed in your RSS feed reader.

You want to be able to make it as easy as possible for people to return regularly to read your blog content. To help your readers do this, place an RSS icon in the top right-hand part of your blog layout. (Remember to link your blog feed's URL to the RSS icon.) Some people would prefer to have your new blog posts delivered straight to their inbox. A free service, such as Google Feedburner, will let you offer that facility to your blog readers.

Summary

A blog is a form of website where you can self-publish articles without needing the approval of anyone else. Anyone can start up a blog in minutes using a free blogging tool such as WordPress or Blogger.

In the world of online networking, your blog is your main tool to demonstrate your credibility with your target audience and strengthen your online personal brand.

The point of a blog is to help people see past the commercial literature and help connect with you as a person.

A blog is an effective networking tool only if you have a mechanism for people to know about your blog and want to come and read it. An effective mechanism is to use online networking sites, such as Twitter, Facebook, Google+ or LinkedIn, to publicise your blog.

Use an RSS feed reader to access all your favourite blogs in one place. Include an RSS feed icon within your blog's layout to allow your readers to subscribe to your blog's RSS feed.

ACTION POINTS

■ Find three well-written blogs aimed at your target market and regularly read them and comment on the blog posts.

■ Start your own blog or start contributing to your firm's blog.

■ Brainstorm with others potential subjects for your blog or your firm's blog.

■ Ask your clients which blogs they regularly read and what they would find of benefit in a blog.

■ Set up Google Feedburner for your blog, and put a 'subscribe to this blog' option – via either email or RSS feeder – in the top right-hand part of your blog's layout.

Further resources

Books

Clapperton, G., *This is Social Media: Tweet, blog, link and post your way to business success*, Capstone, 2009.

Jefferson, S. and Tanton, S., *Valuable Content Marketing*, Kogan Page, 2013.

Rowse, D. and Garrett, C., *ProBlogger: Secrets for blogging your way to a six-figure income*, John Wiley & Sons, 3rd edn, 2012.

Schawbel, D., *Me 2.0: Build a powerful brand to achieve career success*, Kaplan Trade, revised edn, 2010.

Thewlis, P., *WordPress for Business Bloggers*, Packt Publishing, 2008.

Websites and blogs

Joined up Business Networking www.joinedupnetworking.com

Valuable Content www.valuablecontent.co.uk

Blogging software

Drupal www.drupal.org

Blogger www.blogger.com

Wordpress wordpress.org and wordpress.com

3

Essential networking skills for the joined-up networker

So far in the book we've looked at where to network, and the behaviours and attitudes needed to be a great networker. In the next part of the book, we are going to look at the skills needed when networking.

7

An introduction to the FITTER™ process for successful networking

What topics are covered in this chapter?

- A simple networking model to help you network in a time-efficient manner
- What research you can do to help you prepare for a networking event
- How to categorise your network and focus your energy on the people who really matter to you
- How you can follow up effectively after a networking event

'Networking takes a lot of your time and energy – and yet so many people simply go along and see what happens.'

Bryony Thomas, author of Watertight Marketing

Many professionals, when networking, have pleasant conversations which lead precisely nowhere. Networking without purpose, focus or results ends up being a massive waste of time and money. This is the reason I devised the FITTER™ model. I have developed the model over the past few years and used it to train professionals on how to network in a time-efficient manner. This model gives you a simple mnemonic, which will enable you to network efficiently and effectively anywhere and any time.

What is the FITTER™ model?

The FITTER™ mnemonic is not a step-by-step process – you need to be mindful of doing *all* of these things *all* of the time when networking.

FITTER™ stands for:

Follow up

Introduce yourself with impact

Target specific people

Turn social conversations into business chat

Engage

Research

Follow up

'Similar to a golfer, the follow through for networkers is as important as how you hit the ball.'

Jon Baker, co-author of The Go-To Expert

How many times have you been along to a networking event and had some excellent conversations? Business cards are exchanged with a sincere desire to 'stay in touch'. You get back to work the next day, get stuck in with your client work; the people you met the day before soon become a distant memory and just another business card in the bottom of your drawer.

❝❝After an event, you need to sort the wood from the trees❞❞

Does this sound familiar? Neglecting to follow up after a networking event probably is the biggest mistake professionals make when networking. Failing to follow up turns all your hard effort during the networking event into a waste of your time.

Not everyone you meet will be important to you and your business or career going forward. After an event, you need to sort the wood from the trees, i.e. who is worth spending more time with to develop a stronger relationship.

Tip

Block out an hour in your diary the day after a networking event to follow up your new contacts.

After the event, within 24 hours of meeting someone, sort through the contacts you made and split them into three piles:

■ *A-listers:* these are contacts who are well connected to your target market and are likely to help you immediately achieve your business or career goals, e.g. become a referral source, supplier, introducer or new client.

■ *B-listers:* these are contacts you enjoyed meeting but are unlikely to help you immediately achieve your business or career goals.

■ *C-listers:* these are contacts you met but are very unlikely to help you achieve your business or career goals.

Tip

Spend time with your team, agreeing on who or what makes up an A-, B- or C-lister for each person and the team as a whole. Agree on a process to introduce a new contact to the right member of the team.

Regardless of whether they are an A-, B- or C-lister, every one needs to go into your contacts database, and you should ask to connect with them on Twitter, Google+ and LinkedIn. Even if you don't have specialist relationship management software, most email clients, such as Outlook and Google Contacts, will have the functionality to manage your contacts. Make a note of where you met them. Even if you don't think you'll get in touch, keep a note of the contact – you never know who people know!

Tip

To keep your A-listers visible, create a list for them in Twitter and a tag for them in your relationship management software and on LinkedIn.

When you add a contact, here are details that you should aim to record:

■ name, address, telephone number(s)

■ company name

■ website address

■ Twitter accounts – company and personal

■ LinkedIn profile

- Google+ profile
- their company on LinkedIn
- when and where you met. Additionally, jot some details about them and what you discussed
- a comment to help you remember them if you met them again – e.g. 'Looks a little bit like Sean Connery'.

When you are given someone's business card, always ask their permission to add them to your contact list and ask whether you might be able to send them an email or give them a ring. If you don't get their permission and you add them to your mailing list, you are violating anti-spamming laws in the USA and the UK. If you have gained permission verbally to add a contact to your mailing list, then it is fine to add them when you return to the office.

When following up with your A- and B-listers, think about easy ways you can increase your social capital or credibility with them. For example:

- sending them an article that they will find interesting or useful
- offering to connect them to someone in your network
- sending them a link to a website or blog that will be useful to them.

> **Tip**
>
> If you have a long list of people you want to meet face-to-face, block out a day in your diary and aim to meet them on that day in a local hotel's lounge.

A-listers

Your A-list comprises people who will join the 'inner circle' of your network. These are the people who are most likely to help you achieve your networking objectives, e.g. finding new business or a new job. After meeting an A-lister, you want to strengthen the relationship quickly, which means initiating a meeting – ideally in person, but otherwise via video call or phone call, if a face-to-face meeting is not practical. Ideally, you would have asked already for a further conversation at the event; if not, pick up the phone or send an email, reminding them where you met them and indicating the benefit to them of spending more time with you.

For example:

Hello Robert,

It was great to meet you yesterday at the ICAEW event. I really enjoyed our conversation and would like to find out more about what you do with your clients in the manufacturing sector. That way, if I meet someone who needs your, or your firm's, services, I could recommend you to them.

I'm happy to meet at a location of your choosing. However, there is a great little hotel, Harden Grange, near to the two of us where I tend to meet people. Coffee's on me! My diary is pretty free on Monday or Tuesday next week. Does either of those days work for you?

My phone number is 0777 123 4567. Looking forward to getting to know you better.

Kind regards,

Brian

Tip

For the really important relationship, send a handwritten card or postcard rather than an email, saying how much you enjoyed meeting them. You'll be surprised how many people will keep the card displayed prominently on their desk.

On your relationship management system, set up a recurring task to speak physically to your new A-lister at least once a month. Remember to send a request to connect with them on LinkedIn, stating where you met them. For example:

Hello Robert,

It was great to meet you yesterday at the ICAEW event. As you are a person I would value staying in touch with, I would like to add you to my LinkedIn contacts.

Kind regards,

Brian

'I always personalise my LinkedIn invitations, for example, "It was great to talk to you yesterday", or "Here is the article I promised I would send you". This helps me be memorable and stand out from everyone else they met that day.'

Karen Spillane, training professional

B-listers

Your B-list comprises people who you want to stay in touch with but who are unlikely, in the short term, to be a source of referrals, suppliers, introductions or new clients. However, you never know who they may meet, or what may change. Your aim is to connect with these people by as many touch points as possible, with minimal effort on your part.

> **Tip**
>
> To cut down the amount of time spent sending follow-up emails after an event, set up standard follow-up email templates for A-, B- and C-listers for you and others in your firm to use.

❝Connect with your B-listers on LinkedIn❞

Similar to A-listers, connect with your B-listers on LinkedIn, and set a recurring task to communicate with them at least once every three months. This could be an email, or message on Twitter or LinkedIn – it doesn't need to be a phone call or face-to-face meeting.

Remember to send them a short email, within 48 hours of meeting them, stating how much you enjoyed meeting them and giving them a reason to sign up to your mailing list. For example:

Dear Juliet,

Hello, we met yesterday at the BNI's visitors' day.

I enjoyed our conversation and found your stories about the printing industry fascinating.

I would love to stay in touch, and have sent you a LinkedIn invitation and started to follow you on Twitter (I'm @Sarah_James).

My firm sends out a monthly newsletter to everyone on our mailing list – full of interesting articles and advice for anyone wanting to minimise their tax bill. Anyone who signs up gets a copy of our firm's guide to future tax legislation and what it means for small businesses. If you would like a copy of this, then please click here to sign up to our mailing list.

If there is anything I can help you with, please give me a call.

Kind regards,

Sarah

C-listers

Whilst C-listers are unlikely to be a useful contact for you, it is always worth generating a positive impression by sending them a follow-up email. After all, you never know who they may know. Very few people actually send follow-up emails after an event, and this small act will boost your social capital and credibility. For example:

Dear Juliet,

Hello, we met yesterday at the BNI's visitor's day.

It was good to talk to you, and good luck with your future plans. I've started to follow you on Twitter (I'm @Sarah_James).

Just in case you know anyone who may be interested, my firm sends out a monthly newsletter to everyone on our mailing list – full of interesting articles and advice for anyone wanting to minimise their tax bill. Anyone who signs up gets a copy of our firm's guide to future tax legislation and what it means for small businesses. If you know someone who would benefit from a copy of this, then please forward on this email to them. They will need to click here to sign up to our mailing list.

If there is anything I can help you with, please give me a call.

Kind regards,

Sarah

Introduce yourself with impact

You only ever get one chance to make a great first impression. So it's important to introduce yourself with impact – one that will highlight your credibility and encourage people to engage with you. In Chapter 8 you will discover how to make the right first impression and what to say when asked the question, 'So, what do you do?'

Target specific people

If you've ever been to a networking event, you will know how easy it is to end up having great conversations but not actually talking to the people you have gone to the event to meet. If you have done your homework before an event (see the later section in this chapter on research), you will have a shortlist of five to ten people you want to meet at the event. How many of these people could you contact via LinkedIn or Twitter beforehand and arrange to meet at the event? Perhaps you could get your host to introduce you to them?

'I want to maximise my effectiveness when networking, so I will only sign up for an event when I know that at least three people I want to meet will be there.'

Jay Blake, Business Video Production

Before you attend an event, tweet that you are attending and use your LinkedIn status to let people know you are going, asking whether anyone else is also going. This may encourage someone who wants to meet you or get to know you better to attend the same event. When I tweeted that I was going to attend the tweetup after the Lex 2011 conference, at least two people decided to attend just to meet me. (One of these people then became a client!) Connecting up with people in advance of an event gives you additional purpose to attend the event, as well as the opportunity to strengthen an existing relationship. If you don't already know someone you are meeting, agree a time and location to meet – for example, by the event registration stand.

For more details on how to target specific people, see Chapter 10, 'How to work a room'.

Turn social conversations into business chat

'Don't count conversations, make your conversations count.'

Rob Brown, motivational speaker and networking expert[1]

If you've done your research, you will know what ideally you want to achieve as a result of meeting this person. However, do not fall into the trap of diving straight into business. Blurting out your objective for meeting someone within the first minute of meeting them is very unlikely to be constructive. Before you start talking business, take your time to get to know the person and generate some rapport. See Chapter 9 for more detail on how to generate rapport quickly with everyone.

Some good questions to use to move your conversation into a business-orientated conversation include:

- How's business at the moment?
- What's your ideal client?
- What problems do you solve for your clients?
- How do you market your business?
- What challenges are you facing at the moment?
- Who is your ideal referral source?

---

[1] www.therobbrown.com

Engage

> **❝You are there to start a mutually beneficial relationship❞**

When meeting someone at a networking event, focus 80 per cent of your energy on listening and finding out about them: their objectives for being at the event, who they are, shared hobbies, interests and mutual acquaintances, and what makes them tick. Remember, you are not there to sell; you are there to start a mutually beneficial relationship, which can be accelerated by being able to help them there and then.

For example, how about asking them:

- What has brought them to this event?
- Who are they hoping to meet at the event?
- What do they want to achieve by the end of the event?

Most people, unless they are very self-obsessed, will always reciprocate and find out about you and your agenda. If they don't, do you really want to spend time on someone who is not interested in you?

For more details on how to engage in a conversation, see Chapter 8, 'Making the right first impression' and Chapter 10, 'How to work a room'.

Research

Before you attend a networking event, you need to do your homework. Your research will enable you to focus only on the events worth attending, the people who will be beneficial to you to meet or reconnect with and good topics to talk about. This research can be done for you by your personal assistant. Let's say you are an accountant and are looking for a new job within a private practice locally. Therefore, you want to be meeting partners within local accountancy firms and people well connected to these firms, e.g. partners within law firms. Your research will identify which local events they are likely to turn up to, plus who are the people from the firm you would benefit from an introduction to.

Tip

Use an RSS reader, such as Feedly, to take a feed from websites of organisations that host events you may want to attend. This way you will be informed automatically of good events for you to attend.

Once you know what event you are going to attend, the next stage is to prioritise who you want to meet. Most event organisers will give you a delegate list in advance. See if the event is listed on Google+ or Facebook, and see who has listed themselves as going. If you are on Twitter, tweet that you are going and ask if anyone else is.

> **Tip**
>
> Don't forget to reconnect with existing members of your network at events. Strengthening your network is just as important as extending your network.

After you have a list of people attending the event, it is time to find out as much as you can about the attendees and, crucially, what they look like. Your aim is to have a short list of about five to ten people who you would really like to meet.

Here's how you can find out more about someone:

- Search for them on LinkedIn.
- Look at their company website.
- Do a Google search on their name.
- Search for them on Facebook.
- See whether any of your trusted connections on LinkedIn are connected to them and could tell you more about them.
- See whether they are on Twitter and what they tweet about.

Remember that your aim is to find five to ten target people, and something that you can ask them, which gets them talking to you. It's a great way to make a first impression and quickly build rapport and credibility if you can demonstrate some shared knowledge or connection.

'Hello Lola, I was hoping to meet you here tonight. I think we have a mutual friend in Dwain. May I ask how you met him?'

Spend some time thinking what you would like to achieve as a result of meeting these people. Is it a further meeting, an introduction to someone in their organisation, or a chance to send them an article or report?

Either on the day before the event or the morning of the event, have a quick scan through the news, business and sports sections of the BBC website and industry-related press. This will give you conversation starters at the event and an opportunity to voice your opinion and demonstrate your professional credibility.

Summary

FITTER™ stands for:

Follow up: sort people into A-, B- and C-listers, add them into your database and make contact with them.

Introduce yourself with impact: a good impression will start a mutually good relationship.

Target specific people: your time is precious, so make sure you know who you want to meet and why you want to meet them.

Turn social conversations into business chat: take your time to get to know the person first and then move the conversation on to business topics.

Engage: focus 80 per cent of your energy on listening and finding out about them.

Research: focus only on events worth attending and the people worth meeting.

ACTION POINTS

■ Think about your current business or career objectives. What defines, for you personally, an A-, B- or C-lister? What questions can you ask to help you identify A-listers?

■ Look at your current network. Who are your A-listers? How many of them have you spoken to in the last month? How could you strengthen your relationships with your A-listers?

■ If you already have a contacts database for your network, add in an extra column or field where you can categorise your existing contacts as A-, B- or C-listers. Then review all your existing contacts.

■ Where could you network to start meeting A- or B-listers?

■ What preparation do you complete before you attend a networking event? What could you do to better prepare before you attend an event?

■ Before your next networking event, identify a shortlist of five to ten people you want to meet. What can you find out about them using Google, LinkedIn and Twitter?

■ What processes and systems can you put in place to follow up consistently both with new people you meet and your existing network?

Further resources

Books

Ferrazzi, K., *Never Eat Alone: And other secrets to success, one relationship at a time,* Crown Business, 2005 (expected updated edition June 2014).

Gladwell, M., *The Tipping Point,* Abacus, 40th anniversary edition, 2013.

Websites and blogs

Joined Up Networking www.joinedupnetworking.com

Winning business – the secrets of staying in touch www.winningbusiness.net/downloads/pdfs/InTouch.pdf

8

Making the right first impression

What topics are covered in this chapter?

- How to introduce yourself with impact
- What to put into your 60-second pitch for maximum success
- How to present your best online 'face'

In the last chapter we explored how you can use the FITTER™ model to network efficiently and effectively anywhere and any time. Up to this point in the book, we have been talking about the behaviours, attitudes and ingredients necessary to be successful as a networker. Underpinning these success factors is a networker's ability to make the right first impression. Without a great first impression, the relationship is going to struggle to start. In this chapter we will look at how to make a great and memorable first impression.

How to make the right first impression when meeting people

First impressions are everything. Get it right and everything becomes easy. Get it wrong and you have a hard task ahead of you to correct those all-important first impressions. We humans can't help forming an opinion in a few seconds when we meet a stranger; it's how we are programmed for survival.

So, what do I mean by a great first impression? In both the real and virtual world people respond well to warm, positive and confident folk. If you

❝People respond well to warm, positive and confident folk❞

are meeting someone in person, this means offer your handshake first, give them a warm smile and be positive and enthusiastic. This simple act will convey credibility and a likeable personal brand.

If someone is meeting you for the first time in the virtual world, there isn't the equivalent of a handshake. But don't be fooled, they will still be forming a perception of you from that first meeting. If your answer, tweet or blog post conveys warmth, positivity, authenticity and likeability, then you are halfway there to creating a great first impression. If your first online meeting is positive, the next thing that someone will do is look at your profile, blog or website. This is why it is so important to spend time on your social networking profiles and general web presence.

The Zero Moment of Truth

'The best brands consistently win two moments of truth. The first moment occurs at the shop shelf, when the consumer decides whether to buy one brand or another. The second occurs at home, when she uses the brand – and is delighted, or isn't.'

AG Lafley, P&G CEO

If you are given a recommendation for a supplier, what do you do? Phone them immediately, or check them out first on the internet? You check them out.... Google, in its eBook *Winning the Zero Moment of Truth* by Jim Lecinski, discovered that there is now a new 'moment of truth', the Zero Moment of Truth, in the buying process, which happens before buyers engage with you.

In fact, Hubspot discovered that buyers used 5.3 sources of information in 2009 (and this doubled to 10.4 sources of information in 2010) before formally starting the buying process with a supplier. These sources of information include:

- people similar to myself
- my social networks (online and offline)
- micro-blogging platforms, such as Twitter
- websites that share valuable content.

Consequently, before your potential client/customer (or even recruiter) calls you, they will have done their research on you, and answered the following questions in their mind:

■ What service do I think I actually need?

■ Are you able to deliver that service at the right price?

■ Do I think I can trust you to deliver the service I require, in the way I want it delivered?

If you ignore the online world and focus your networking efforts almost solely in the face-to-face world, you will be missing out on opportunities to generate new business, or even a new role.

The importance of your handshake

What's worse? A palm-shattering, bone crunching handshake? Or being offered a hand that feels more like a limp fish? Originally, handshakes were used to prove that we came in peace and did not have a weapon. Nowadays, we use handshakes all the time – but particularly when meeting and greeting someone.

Handshakes are a sign of trust and help build strong relationships. Your handshake is just one of the ways you can build a positive first impression. Psychologists have found that, if you take the initiative and move forward to meet a person and shake their hand, their impression of you will be more favourable than if you waited for them to take the initiative.

However, handshakes mean different things in different cultures. In today's global marketplace, you could find yourself networking with people from Africa, Japan or the USA. Whereas in the USA a firm handshake equals self-confidence, in Africa a limp handshake is the way to do it. In Africa, expect to be shaking hands for as much as a couple of minutes. In the USA, expect to get some very strange looks if your handshake goes on for more than a few seconds.

I'm guessing that many people don't know the full impact of their handshake – and don't even give their handshake a moment's thought. My suggestion is you need to be aware of the first impression that your handshake portrays. That's right. I'm suggesting that you practise your handshake on people you trust. Sounds embarrassing? It is far better to identify and fix a problem handshake before it impacts on your career or potential to win new business.

Dress for success

How do I put this delicately? Appearances do count, and stereotypes do exist. If you think of a lawyer, you expect to see a well-tailored suit and a neat appearance. As many image consultants will tell you, details are important. Chipped nail polish or dirty nails is a no-no, as is missing buttons from a coat, dirty shoes or messy hair. To give you an analogy, would you return to a shop if it had dirty carpets and dust on the shelf?

If you look good and have a confident handshake, then the battle for the right first impression is nearly won.

Your opening sound bite

The last piece of the jigsaw is how you introduce yourself. For many professionals, a big trap is waiting for them when asked (the almost standard question at a networking event), 'So what do you do?' Do you confess and say, 'I'm an accountant/lawyer/coach?' Or do you describe what you do by the value you bring to your clients? For example, an accountant may describe what they do like this:

'I help my clients legally pay only the right amount of tax, not a penny more, not a penny less.'

The right answer is to have the one-sentence sound bite prepared, which succinctly talks about the value you bring to your clients. This is my opening sound bite:

'I help professionals become the Go-To Expert.'

By talking about the value you bring to your clients early in the conversation, you are emphasising the benefits of your service rather than the features. After all, every sales person will tell you that people buy benefits, not features.

When I train people to use an opening sound bite describing the value they bring to their clients, many worry that the other person won't know what they do. I can see that this is a genuine concern. However, in my experience, whenever this type of opening is used, the next question is, 'Oh, that sounds interesting, how do you do that?' And then you are off, the conversation is started, and you have moved straight into a business conversation. Your aim with the opening sound bite is to pique someone's curiosity so that they want to ask you a question about it.

A networker's pitch

Attend any referral generation club, e.g. a BNI breakfast meeting, or speed networking event, and everyone will be asked to deliver a pitch on behalf of their business. Often this pitch will be the first time that all of the club members have met you. There are many reasons why your pitch needs to be word perfect – and we will discuss these in this chapter – however, your pitch is a point in time when people will be forming a first impression of you. Typically, most networking events limit people's pitches to one minute or less, which is why they are often called 60-second pitches. A well-delivered and thought-out pitch will encourage club members to help you and interact with you.

In essence, these pitches are your opportunity to talk about your business and ask the other people at the meeting for help to achieve your networking objectives. Your networking pitch is the only time when networking that you are allowed to sell!

A successful pitch has the following characteristics:

■ It is short and punchy and keeps strictly to the time limit.

■ It engages the audience by starting with a question.

■ It is specific in who or what help is wanted from the group, i.e. a call to action.

■ It demonstrates your credibility.

■ It talks about only one feature of your service.

■ It repeats your name twice with features of your service, as it helps people to remember you.

■ It is memorable.

What should go into your pitch?

Your aim with a pitch is to encourage people to take action and think about who within their networks can help you. Often in networking circles you will hear this called 'selling through the room' rather than 'selling to the room'. If there are 10 people in the room listening to your pitch, and each of them has a good network of more than 100 people, then if you 'sell through the room', i.e. to each of their networks, rather than to each of the people in the room directly, you have a greater probability of success.

> **Tip**
>
> Plan your pitch in advance and in conjunction with your marketing plan.

In the FITTER™ model we talked about targeting specific people. When preparing your pitch, first you need to think about what you are trying to achieve by being at that networking event, e.g. who are you looking to meet? The more specific you are about who you want to meet, the more quality introductions and referrals you will receive. Perhaps more importantly, who are you representing? Some networkers have several business interests and need to decide, when they are out networking, which business they are representing. Sixty seconds is too short to try to 'pitch' two businesses – it will only confuse the audience. For example, there will be times when I want to actively push our coaching services to small professional practices, and other times that I will want to emphasise our big firm credentials. Before I go to an event where I will have to deliver a 60-second pitch, I will decide which part of our business I am promoting to the event.

> **Tip**
>
> Think about using a prop, e.g. a picture, for your pitch. It will help to make you more memorable.

Next, think about what client pain you solve with your services. What example can you think of to highlight your credibility at solving your client's problems, e.g. a client testimonial or recent case study? Include evidence of the benefits your product or service brought to your client.

> **Tip**
>
> To help calm your nerves before delivering your pitch, visualise yourself delivering the pitch perfectly, with everyone listening intently.

Here is a simple structure for you to use to put together your pitch:

1 Say your name, the name of your company and the value you bring to your clients; make it a question rather than a statement:

   Hello, my name is Heather Townsend and I help professionals become the Go-To Expert. Would you like to generate more business via referral in less time?

2 Then who you work with:

We work exclusively with professional advisors, such as lawyers, accountants and consultants.

3 Then talk about something that demonstrates your credibility:

Over the last year I have been coaching a 2-partner, 40-strong practice to double their revenue and profit from £2 million to £4 million. As a result of restructuring their management team and giving them the skills they needed to step up, they have found that, in just one year, they are 50 per cent of the way towards their 3-year targets.

4 What you are looking for:

This week I am looking for lawyers and accountants whose 1–4 partner practice is growing rapidly and are finding that they don't have the right team around them to carry on their growth. Who do you know who fits this description?

5 Repeat your name and your business:

I'm Heather Townsend and I help professionals become the Go-To Expert. Would you like to generate more business via referral in less time?

Tip

Keep the messages of your pitch consistent but vary the content of your pitch, so your regular audience has a reason to listen to your pitch week in, week out.

Many well-attended referral generation clubs will let members have only 40 seconds for their pitch. For example, this is the short pitch that Jon Baker, my business partner, uses:

'My name is Jon Baker and I help owners of small professional practices enjoy the freedom and lifestyle that comes with an income of over £150,000 from their business. Do you find that you have too many clients to focus more on your marketing? But not enough leads coming into your business to achieve your growth plans? We typically help our accountancy, legal and consultancy clients double or triple the number of leads they receive each month.

I am looking for introductions to local professional practices who have partners retiring and new young partners taking over from them.

I am Jon Baker and I help owners of small professional practices enjoy the freedom and lifestyle that comes with an income of over £150,000 from their business.'

> **Tip**
>
> When you are new to a referral generation club, use your pitch to showcase your credibility and build up trust, rather than ask for business.

There are many different ways to establish your credibility in your pitch, for example:

- Talk about what you have achieved for your clients in the last few weeks.

- Describe how you went the extra mile for a client.

- Mention new client wins and why they chose you.

- Quote a client testimonial.

- Chat about any recent PR, award wins or good stuff that has happened.

- Speak with confidence, as your audience is wanting to see that you are confident in your product or service and that you can deliver to time and the right level of quality.

- Keep your message consistent.

Your online footprint

> **Tip**
>
> When writing your profile in Twitter, include the people who you would like to follow you. Many people use search tools to find people with certain words in their profile.

The online equivalent of a networking pitch and opening sound bite is your online profile or biography. When someone connects with you online and likes what they see, the first thing they normally read is your profile or online biography. Their reason? It's to find out more about you and evaluate whether you are the type of person they want to get to know. This may sound callous, but, every time you meet someone new in person, you are deciding subconsciously whether you want to get to know them better. This may be only the quick decision whether to follow someone on Twitter, or it may be a decision to contact them with a view to hiring them in the future.

> **Tip**
>
> Use a professionally taken head-and-shoulders shot of yourself for your online picture. Don't use your company's logo, as people want to meet you, not your company.

❝It is important to include keywords in your profile❞

Your online presence needs to include a professional head-and-shoulders shot of you, and should also demonstrate your credibility and position your brand, e.g. state who you work with, and the problems that you solve for your clients. Very often a social networking site, e.g. LinkedIn, and the profiles within it are rated very highly by Google. Therefore, to help you appear near the top of the search engine rankings for content you control, it is important to include keywords in your profile that your clients are likely to be searching for online.

> **Tip**
>
> To keep your private life truly private on Facebook, untag yourself from incriminating photos and set your privacy settings to the highest level.

When we meet someone in person, very often our instinct tells us whether we can trust them or not. When we meet someone online, we can rely only on the written word and what their photo looks like. Trust is generated in online relationships often by consistency, i.e. answering the same types of questions, tweeting on similar themes and having the same profile and professional-looking photo, regardless of which online networking site you meet people on.

What needs to go in your online biography or profile

Your online biography, or bio, is part of your networking toolkit. You need to have a couple of versions of your online biography prepared, for example:

- to use as an author credit for your articles
- to use within marketing materials, for example if you are a guest speaker
- to use in your social networking site's profiles, e.g. Twitter and LinkedIn.

> **Tip**
>
> Ask your photographer to supply you with both high- and low-resolution versions of your professional head-and-shoulders photo. The high-resolution version should be supplied for printed materials and the low-resolution version should be used online.

Your basic biography needs to consist of your professional head-and-shoulders photo, one sentence stating what you do, then a paragraph qualifying your credibility. For example, here is my basic biography. As an aside I have written my bio here in the third person. It depends on how or where your bio will be used. However, on many social networking sites the accepted etiquette is in the first person rather than third person.

My one sentence stating what I do:

Heather Townsend helps professionals become the Go-To Expert.

My paragraph qualifying my credibility:

Unusually for someone with an Engineering Degree, she accidentally became a writer and used her knowledge on social media to write the current best-selling and award-winning book on networking, The FT Guide to Business Networking. *Heather has also co-authored two more books,* How to Make Partner and Still Have a Life, *and her latest book,* The Go-To Expert: How to grow your reputation, differentiate yourself from the competition and win new business. *People frequently talk about her as someone who really knows her stuff – which may be the reason she has, over the last decade, worked with over 300 partners, and coached and trained over 2,000 professionals at every level of the UK's most ambitious professional practices.*

Some tips when writing your basic biography:

■ Keep it short and sweet: less is more.
■ Don't claim to be more than three things, as it damages your credibility.
■ Include links back to your website and blog.
■ For social networking profiles, especially LinkedIn, include keywords within your profile.

Summary

First impressions are everything. Get it right, and everything becomes easy. When answering the question 'So what do you do?', always answer with the value you bring to your clients, not your occupation or job title.

At a formal networking event, it is vital to prepare a short, punchy but well-thought-out pitch.

Your aim with a pitch is to establish your credibility, be memorable and encourage people to think about who within their networks can help you.

Your online profile needs to be as professional as your personal presence in a networking meeting.

Prepare several versions of your online biography, which state what you do and qualify your credibility.

ACTION POINTS

▦ Ask for feedback on your normal handshake – does it convey the right first impression? Practise on a friend until you get it right.

▦ Next time you are out at a networking event, aim to be the person who initiates a conversation and leans forward to shake hands. Notice how you are treated differently when doing this.

▦ Write out your opening sound bite by describing in one sentence the value you (or your business) bring to your clients. Test out this sound bite next time you are meeting new people at a networking event.

▦ Look at your company's marketing plan. How can you use your networking pitch to help make your company's marketing campaigns a success?

▦ Watch an established networker deliver their pitch. What do they do well? What can you copy?

▦ What props could you use to strengthen your impact next time you deliver your pitch?

▦ Before you attend your next networking event, take the time to practise your pitch before you deliver it. How does this help improve your impact at the event?

▦ Ask for some feedback on your pitch next time you deliver it. Find out what you can do to improve your impact.

▦ Ask for some feedback on the professional photo that you use on your social networking profiles. Do you look open, warm and welcoming?

▦ If you don't have a professional photo on your online profiles, organise a photo shoot with a professional photographer.

▦ Write your basic online biography. Keep it to one sentence describing what you do, then one short paragraph qualifying your credibility and expertise.

▦ Read your online profiles and biographies – critique them for consistency and credibility. If you don't feel confident in your writing abilities, how about hiring a copywriter to write them for you?

Further resources

Books

D'Souza, S., *Brilliant Networking: What the best networkers know, do and say* Prentice Hall, 2nd edn, 2010.

Lindenfield, G. and Lindenfield, S., *Confident Networking for Career Success and Satisfaction*, Piatkus Books, 2010.

Misner, I.R., Alexander, D.C. and Hilliard, B., *Networking Like a Pro: Turning contacts into connections*, Entrepreneur Press, 2010.

Schawbel, D., *Me 2.0: Build a powerful brand to achieve career success*, Kaplan Trade, revised edn, 2010.

Blogs and websites

Joined Up Business Networking www.joinedupnetworking.com

Dan Schawbel's 'Personal Branding' blog www.personalbrandingblog.com

9

How to keep the conversation going

What topics are covered in this chapter?

- How to generate rapport with anyone you meet
- How to recognise the three different communication styles: think, feel, know
- How to have a productive conversation with everyone you meet

In the last chapter we showed you how to make that all-important first impression. But then what happens? How do you go from meeting someone to building a relationship? A connection becomes a positive relationship only when the two of you have rapport and the conversation flows easily. In this chapter we introduce the three different communication styles: think, feel and know. Using these, you can flex your personal style to quickly recognise and build rapport with people with different styles, regardless of whether you are meeting them in person, virtually or via a phone/ video call.

What do we mean by rapport?

People like people who are like themselves or who behave like them. Sensing that someone else is like you is done at the conscious and subconscious (or unconscious) level. Two people who sense that each is like the other at an unconscious level are said to be 'in rapport'. Having an awareness of the conditions needed to generate rapport enables you to adjust your personal style to consciously build rapport with everyone you meet. Ultimately, it is how you choose to communicate that informs the subconscious decision of whether someone will like you or not.

> ### Tip
>
> When you meet someone for the first time, find something that you can compliment them on sincerely.

❝ Mirroring happens naturally when you have generated rapport ❞

Many textbooks and training workshops will teach you a technique called mirroring. This is where you copy the other person's body language, to try to build rapport. Whilst this sounds fine in theory, in practice it never works. In fact, mirroring happens naturally when you have generated rapport, rather than rapport being generated because you have copied someone's gestures.

case study   Hamish Taylor

Hamish Taylor was leading a team from ICI who were meeting with a team from Procter & Gamble to investigate ways of sharing and collaborating on innovative products and technologies. Before the meeting Hamish had looked up every Procter & Gamble-er and identified what their particular expertise and interests were. He used this information to tailor parts of his presentation to connect with each individual member of the Procter & Gamble team's personal agendas. Unsurprisingly, this research was instrumental in setting the stage for a productive meeting.

During the meeting, Hamish overheard a senior Procter & Gamble executive remark, 'I've never met or heard of this Hamish guy before.' Upon hearing this, Hamish quickly re-read the dossier he had compiled on him as an individual. When an occasion presented itself, Hamish took the opportunity to talk with the senior executive. After a few minutes of small talk, Hamish started talking about his time in Japan and how much he had admired the way that Procter & Gamble had dealt with the aftermath of the Kobe earthquake. This was no chance remark, as Hamish knew that this person had been the one directly 'shaken up' by that earthquake. This shared interest, and subsequent conversation, led to a very strong friendship and mutually beneficial relationship between the two of them.

It was the rapid establishment of rapport, as well as the depth of rapport, that led to strong ties between the two teams. The subsequent joint collaboration between the two teams enabled Hamish's subsidiary of ICI's business with Procter & Gamble to grow from $10 million to $70 million in less than five years.

How do people choose to communicate?

Picture the scenario of two people meeting at a networking event. One person asks the other,

'So, what do you do?'

There are three different styles of response:

1   The other person replies with thoughtful, paced and structured detail about what they actually do. For example:

'I do three things. First I am a holistic financial planner for my company, Safe Financial Services. This takes up all my working time. I'm also a husband and father to my two children, Aggie and James, and once a week I volunteer at my local church.'

2   The other person is ready to unburden everything they do. They seem to go on and on, with high amounts of energy, lots of stories and animated gestures. For example:

'I love what I do! One of my clients described me the other day as a "money-saver", but another client recently described me as "guardian of his finances". Personally, I always get a real buzz when I can see a client who I signed up, achieving their financial goals. I don't feel as if I am a financial advisor, as that sounds rather boring...'

3   The other person answers in a succinct, straightforward, calm way, often using only one word or one sentence. For example:

'I'm a financial advisor for Safe Financial Services.'

Each of these three different responses is sending a signal about how the person prefers to be communicated with. These three responses are typical of the three different communication styles.

Response	Style	Attuned to
1	Think	Data
2	Feel	Energy
3	Know	Gut instinct

The three different communication styles

People communicate information based on the way we use the three innate communication styles of *thinking*, *feeling* and *knowing*. No one style is better than another. We all can use all three styles, but we tend to have a preference for one or two styles.

Your aim as a networker is to be able to have a meaningful conversation with every person you meet, and to strengthen the relationship between the two of you. If you meet someone who shares the same communication style preference as yourself, then rapport will develop naturally; however, there is no guarantee that you will have a productive conversation.

Personally, I have an equally strong preference for *feel* and *know*. However, it depends on who I am with, where I am and how I am feeling at the time, whether the *feel* or the *know* will dominate my communication style. If you can spot someone's natural preference for a communication style, by adapting your style to theirs you will reduce miscommunication and promote rapport. In written communication, such as emails, blogs, online forms, your connection and relationship will be improved if you adapt to the primary preference of your target.

Think

> **People with a preference for *think* like to receive data**

People with a preference for *think* like to receive data, absorb all the details and process information in a methodical and logical way. They like to have all the facts before acting.

Thinking communication tends to be in the form of numbers, data and facts. It comprises lengthy processes of thinking through issues. Typically, every step and thought is shared.

If you asked someone with a primary *think* communication preference:

'So, how's business?'

they would tend to respond something like this:

'I need to tell you seven things about my business (Pause for thought)...'

and, whether you like it or not, they will tell you in whole paragraphs what those seven points are.

To build rapport with a think communication style

Use whole paragraphs, structures, logic, detail.

To have a productive conversation with someone who has a think preference

When you meet someone with a *think* preference, often they will appear thoughtful and will be very structured and detailed. If you don't have a *think* preference, the level of detail being communicated can seem inconsequential and boring. Someone with a *know* preference soon will get frustrated when communicating with a *think* preference, as it will feel as if they don't get to the point or, even worse, don't appear to listen to you.

To build the relationship and keep a meaningful conversation flowing:

■ Put structure into your conversation, e.g.

   'There are three things I'm going to tell you about my business. I will tell you about the background of the business, the services we offer, and some recent success stories from our clients.'

■ Ask at the beginning of the conversation what they want to get out of the conversation.

■ Signpost your intentions, e.g.

   'I would love to spend 5–10 minutes finding out more about you and your business.'

■ Ask what it would be helpful for them to know about you and your business.

■ Summarise regularly for them.

■ Be patient and let them get the detail out.

Feel

People with a preference for *feel* are attuned to other people's energy and consider this before making decisions. They empathise with others and are sensitive to their moods. They tend to communicate in stories. They will use visual language, analogies, colours and verbs.

Feeling communication relates how an individual *feels* in or about a situation. The best example of this is walking into a meeting where you can almost 'cut the air with a knife' – this is a feeling.

If you ask someone with a *feel* preference at a networking event:

'So, how's business?'

they are likely to respond in two different ways – depending on whether they are having a good day or a bad day:

'Everything's fantastic, amazing, a little bit frantic – let me paint a picture of my day for you – and let me tell you how I helped my client this week...'

accompanied by an animated face and lots of hand gestures.

Or,

'Business is pretty pants at the moment, and I don't know why I keep on trying to push water uphill with a sieve. If I'm honest, I don't know why I came out tonight.'

To build rapport with a feel communication style

Summarise and show empathy, and aim to relate to the other person's underlying meanings and motivation.

To have a productive conversation with someone who has a feel communication style

> **"Keeping a conversation going with someone with a *feel* preference is never hard"**

When you meet someone with a *feel* preference, they tend to have a lot to say. Their emotions are always near to the surface and, normally, you are left in no doubt as to what they feel about something. To someone with a *think* or a *know* preference, someone with a *feel* preference can seem disjointed and go off on tangents. If someone with a *feel* preference is nervous, the stories may seem to be told for stories' sake. Keeping a conversation going with someone with a *feel* preference is never hard – but getting a word in edgeways or keeping the conversation focused may not be easy!

If you meet someone with a *feel* preference, to keep the conversation flowing and build the relationship:

■ Summarise what they are saying.

■ Use stories, analogies and metaphors.

■ Search for common values, interests and motivations – people with a *feel* communication preference need to feel a connection.

■ Keep the conversation focused and, if necessary, interrupt to bring them back 'on topic'.

Know

People with a preference for *know* take a position and make decisions quickly. Sometimes they are unable to explain that decision, which is based on their gut instinct. Very often their answers to questions will be short and succinct.

Knowing communication is instinctive. *Know* preferences can come across in a harsh manner at times, especially to people with *feel* and *think* preferences, who prefer to express themselves with more words and description.

If you ask someone with a *know* preference at a networking event:

'So, how's business?'

they are likely to respond:

'Good – keeping busy.'

To build rapport with a know communication style

Use short sentences and questions encouraging them to elaborate. Always get to the point quickly, and be succinct.

To have a productive conversation with someone who has a know communication style

These people can be very self-contained and relationship-building behaviours, for example indulging in small talk, may not always be apparent. This self-containment, coupled with a potential lack of relationship-building conversations, can make someone with a strong *know* preference come across as rude and arrogant. The challenge when you meet someone with an apparent *know* preference is to keep the conversation going and get them to elaborate enough to find areas of shared interest. Unlike people with a *feel* preference, people with a *know* preference often are happy to sit in silence. When you meet someone with a *know* preference you may come away from the conversation feeling that you haven't connected – but persevere, as the person with a strong preference for *know*, as opposed to someone with a strong *think* or *feel* preference, can take longer to bond with others.

> **Tip**
>
> If you have met someone and the conversation is not flowing, even though you think you are asking the right questions, there is a strong likelihood that they have a preference for 'know'.

If you meet someone with a *know* preference, to keep the conversation flowing and build the relationship:

■ Ask open questions which extract details, e.g.

'What are you looking to get out of the event today?'

'What does your business do?'

'Was there anyone here you particularly wanted to meet? If so, why?'

■ Keep the conversation focused – don't ramble, and keep to the point.

■ Don't worry if there is an occasional silence or pause in the conversation.

■ Check in regularly with them to ensure that the conversation is beneficial for them.

The ThinkFeelKnow© indicator

If you are interested in finding out what your natural communication style is or helping your team to understand their natural communication styles, there is an easy-to-complete ThinkFeelKnow© indicator profiling tool. This tool provides a personalised online report for people profiling their preferences for the three communication styles. The ThinkFeelKnow© indicator can be accessed via www.thinkfeelknow.com.

Think about five people you work with closely and, using your knowledge about the ThinkFeelKnow© indicator, identify what you think is their natural communication style. Is it *think, feel* or *know*? When you meet them next, change your normal style of communication to match theirs and see what changes as a result.

How to find areas of common interest

❝You need to start with small talk❞

Every productive conversation needs to start somewhere. First, you need to find someone to talk to, then you have to get the conversation going. Before you can develop a conversation so that it becomes a meaningful experience, you need to start with small talk. Joining people in the queue for food or at the bar is a great way to start small talk with someone. It's easy to comment on something to do with the situation you are in, for example:

'The food looks fantastic tonight.'

'Bang goes my diet for today!'

'What takes your fancy on the menu this lunchtime?'

'I'm looking forward to a cold drink. What are you having?'

The purpose of small talk in this instance is to get the conversation started safely. Good positions to stand where you won't be short of someone to talk to are:

■ near the drinks table

■ by the seating plan

■ near the entrance.

If you don't fancy waiting until someone comes to find you, all you need to do is catch someone's eye and smile at them. I promise you, they will come over and talk to you.

One of the best ways to keep the conversation going beyond small talk is to use and listen for relationship hooks. Relationship hooks are where you give an extra bit of detail in order to expand your conversation. For example, instead of saying, *'Good,'* when someone asks you about your day, how about saying, *'Good, but looking forward to the match this evening'*. This then may lead to a long conversation about your mutual shared interest in a team or competitive sport.

Whilst speaking to random people at networking events is all part of the fun of networking, it pays to share your goals early with the people you are meeting – particularly with people who have a *know* communication preference. This way, you will find out quickly how much time you should invest in the conversation. These questions can help you safely share your personal objectives for the event:

'What are you looking to achieve here today?'

'What made you decide to come to this conference?'

Good questions to keep the conversation going

- What prompted you to become a...?
- How's business?
- What's your ideal client?
- What does the future hold for you/your business?
- What have you been enjoying watching recently on TV?
- What are your interests outside of work?
- Have you always lived around here?
- What prompted you to set up your own business?
- What are you enjoying listening to/watching at the moment?
- What sports do you enjoy watching or playing?

Summary

By generating rapport, you are on your way to establishing a mutually beneficial relationship.

There are three communication styles: think, feel, know. To build rapport, you need to learn how to spot the style of other people and then interact with them in a similar style.

Think	Thoughtful, precise, paragraphs, lots of words, numbers
Feel	High energy, passion, visual language, colours, verbs, stories, analogies
Know	Self-contained, calm, headings, short sharp answers – 'bullet points'

Your aim, once you have introduced yourself, is to generate a conversation where you can explore and identify areas of common interest and value.

ACTION POINTS

■ Next time you are out working the room, aim to see whether you can find business or personal contacts you have in common with someone. Notice how the level of rapport changes between the two of you when you have established a mutual contact.

■ Identify your communication style preference by completing the ThinkFeelKnow© indicator at www.thinkfeelknow.com.

■ Think about your close circle of friends – who has a preference for *think*, *feel* and *know*?

■ Find someone you know with a different communication preference to you. Have a go at adapting your style to match theirs. Observe how the conversation flows more freely between the two of you.

Further resources

Books

Benjamin, S., *Perfect Phrases for Professional Networking*, McGraw-Hill Professional, 2009.

D'Souza, S., *Brilliant Networking: What the best networkers know, do and say*, Prentice Hall, 2nd edn, 2010.

Blogs and websites

Joined Up Networking blog www.joinedupnetworking.com

ThinkFeelKnow www.thinkfeelknow.com

Think Feel Know is an international coaching and training company operating in the UK, USA and Australia, dedicated to the understanding and development of people. The Think Feel Know Model and Indicator are protected by Copyright © 2010 Think Feel Know Ltd. All Rights Reserved. Think Feel Know Limited is a company registered in the British Virgin Islands, registered number 1430938. For further information on Think Feel Know and how to apply it personally or within a business environment please visit www.thinkfeelknow.com

Winning business – the secrets of developing great rapport www.winningbusiness.net/downloads/pdfs/Rapport.pdf

10

How to work a room

What topics are covered in this chapter?

- How to overcome nerves when meeting new people
- How to find the right people to talk to at a networking event
- How to circulate effortlessly and break into and out of conversations
- What to take with you when networking
- How to maximise your effectiveness when having a one-to-one meeting
- The etiquette of exchanging business cards

In the last chapter we showed you how to strike up a meaningful conversation with anyone you meet. In this chapter we will show you how to effortlessly find the right people to talk to in a room, so you can have that meaningful conversation.

There is a skill to working the room; however, this skill can be learned. You may be interested to know that a study of social fears undertaken in the USA identified that 'meeting new people in an unfamiliar environment' is nearly as stressful as unrehearsed public speaking.[1]

---

[1] www.ncbi.nlm.nih.gov/pmc/articles/PMC2262178/?tool=pubmed

Five ways to get the right attitude to 'work the room'

1 What is your mind telling you?

If you got a call now telling you that you were going to be attending a networking event this evening, what would be going through your mind?

I strongly suspect some of these thoughts:

- I wonder who will be there?
- I hope I don't bump into this person.
- Please don't let me get stuck with the networking cling-on.
- Let this event be over as quickly as possible so I can get back to work.
- Please let it be better than last week.
- I could really do with generating some good leads and introductions from this event.
- I'm poor at memorising names; I wonder whose name I will forget this time.
- I hope I don't meet one of those networkers who will sell to me.

In effect, whether we like it or not, we have a little voice in our head that is always talking to us. It may be recalling memories, imagining the future, or indulging in self-talk about ourselves, others or the situation. Sometimes this little voice can be helpful and sometimes downright unhelpful. The question is, how much do you listen to this voice as you are preparing, or even working, the room?

For example, are you really poor at memorising names? Or do you just tell yourself you are, so there is no point in taking the time to remember them? (I heard this one recently!)

2 Ditch the burden of feeling you need to sell

Another burden many of us take into a networking event is the pressure to generate leads. It is amazing how often we trick ourselves into believing that we can go to a networking event and, based on one quick five-minute conversation, win invoiceable business. Logically, if you sell a high-priced service or product, this just won't happen. At best, you may meet someone who may need your services or can introduce you to someone who needs your services. However, you still need to spend time developing the relationship and your credibility before the lead becomes a true lead rather than a prospect.

If you head into the room feeling like you need to sell, it is amazing how poor your experience can be when you are networking. If you head into the room focused on having a couple of quality conversations and meeting the people you planned to, often it is a very different experience when you work the room. Your aim is to find the right relationships to spend time nurturing and building – not look for potential clients in the room.

3 Challenge the self-limiting beliefs

Very often our negative self-talk is driven by our self-limiting beliefs – i.e. things your subconscious tells you in order to protect you, but which limit your potential. These self-limiting beliefs may be based on a previous bad experience when networking, or may not. Some of the common self-limiting beliefs I hear about are:

- I struggle to keep conversations going.
- I am bad at memorising names.
- I always get stuck with the networking bore.
- I'm poor at starting conversations.

If you hold these thoughts in your head when you go and work a room, is it any wonder that you find yourself struggling to effortlessly work a room?

4 Be in the right room

So many people turn up to the wrong events. I don't mean that they walk into the wrong room at the venue; I mean that they are going to events where they are unlikely to meet the sort of people that they want to meet when networking. If you find yourself networking for networking's sake, then probably you are turning up in the wrong rooms. It is amazing how much confidence and positivity you can get by knowing that the right people that you need to meet are at the same event as you.

5 Arrive ready to network

I see this happening so often with professionals and busy business owners when they are networking. They rush off from a meeting to the networking event. Then they rush off from the networking event to the next thing in their busy calendar. As a result, they arrive flustered, leave flustered and never quite manage to get in any of those deeper and longer conversations that lead to the right interations and relationships being had. Next time you head out to 'work a room', leave some breathing space in your diary to arrive refreshed, relaxed and mentally alert.

Overcoming nerves

'When meeting a stranger, and worrying whether you will be able to keep the conversation going, remember SW3 – Some Will, Some Won't, So What!'

Girish Shah, senior finance manager

Not everyone enjoys meeting new people. In fact, many professionals avoid attending networking events because of their dread and fears about meeting new people. Very often people are scared of rejection, or not knowing what to say. For example:

'What if I don't know what to say?'

'What if I get stuck in a conversation with someone very boring?'

'What happens if I can't find anyone to talk to?'

Most of these fears are not grounded in reality and are self-limiting beliefs. There are many ways to overcome these nerves, for example:

- Visualise yourself, before an event, having an enjoyable and fun time meeting new people.
- Arrange to meet a friend or colleague at the event – but agree to split up and circulate.
- Commit to attend a networking event regularly, as the more experience you have of working the room, the easier it becomes.
- Practise your 'working the room' skills at big 'safe' social events.
- Surf the news sites on the internet and find some topics that you would find interesting to discuss with people you meet, such as *'What do you think of the government's planned changes to...?'*
- Remember that everyone who goes out networking is in the same position as you – they want to meet new people and have interesting conversations.

Finding the right people to talk to

❝People expect to meet people and circulate❞

The rules of a business gathering are different from a social gathering. People expect to meet people and circulate, and won't be offended if you don't want to stay by their side all through the event. In fact, the very opposite is true – they may get very frustrated if you cling to them like a limpet all through the event.

If you position yourself so that you can see people entering the room, you will be able to quickly spot friends, contacts, clients – even people you want to avoid! But here is the twist: you will be able to see people without seemingly breaking rapport or focus on the person you are talking to. There is nothing more off-putting than someone twisting their head to look around the room when they are talking to you.

If you have come specifically to meet a person, the best way to make sure this happens is to contact them before the event and arrange a time and place to meet, such as over lunch or during the first seminar session. Failing that, ask your event's host to introduce you to the person you want to meet.

At most business gatherings there is normally a formal part of the proceedings, be it a seminar, speaker or meal. You want to be selective about who you sit down with, and strengthen your relationship with, during this part of the proceedings.

Five minutes before the sit-down part of an event starts, ask your host to introduce you to one of the people you have come to the event to meet. After speaking to them for a few minutes, you then simply say, '*I'm enjoying our conversation, may I join you for the...?*'

If you've made the right impression, the answer normally will be 'Yes' and you now have a huge opportunity to build upon your initial conversation and develop a deeper relationship during the formal event proceedings.

Why you need to circulate

As a busy professional or business owner you need to get the most out of your networking time. Whilst networking should be fun and enjoyable, you need to be focused on what you planned to achieve at the event. This means you need to be evaluating the usefulness of each conversation you are having.

You may be having a very enjoyable conversation comparing notes on your new shoes with someone you have just met, but, if they are unlikely in the short or medium term to help you meet your goals, then this becomes just a cosy conversation. The more time you spend having cosy conversations or speaking to random people not on your list, the less time you will have available to speak to the people you have come here to meet. Everyone at a networking event has come with the purpose of meeting people. So, no one will be offended if you don't talk to them for the whole evening. Whilst there is nothing wrong with having only one or two really positive and engaging conversations at an event, you have missed out on the opportunity to speak to a whole room full of potential A-listers.

Normally about 5–10 minutes into a conversation you will know whether this is a useful connection or just a pleasant chat. At this point you need to make a decision before you break off the conversation and recirculate: is this person an A-lister or a B-lister and therefore worth asking to meet up for a one-to-one in the future? If you think this person has the potential to become an A-lister for you, then spend a little longer getting to know them before asking to meet up for a one-to-one.

Tip

Maybe you've gone networking with someone else for moral support, but you will achieve more if you break up and tackle the room individually. You can come back together at certain points and swap information and contacts that you have made.

I attend face-to-face networking events regularly and continue to be amazed by the number of people from the same company standing talking to each other. Why waste valuable networking time when they could have had that conversation in the office?

By dividing and conquering, a team of you can network with everyone in the room rather than just talking to the one or two brave souls who come up and talk with the gaggle of you in the corner.

Exiting from a conversation

The most common question I get asked when I run a talk or workshop on networking, is 'How do I exit from a conversation – particularly if I have got stuck with the networking bore?' There is a technique to exiting gracefully from a conversation. First you want to signal to the person you are talking to that the conversation is about to end. The best way of doing this is to say something along the lines of:

'It's been great talking to you. Do you have a business card?'

Then the golden rule is never to leave someone on their own. The best way to do this, and build up your social capital at the same time, is to introduce them to someone else and then make your excuses to leave. If no one comes to rescue you, there is nothing stopping you going to find another person to introduce to them – for example, in the queue for the drinks or the buffet. Or you could ask them who they would like to meet at the event and then aim to connect them.

Always aim to give a plausible reason to exit, for example 'Nature calls' or that you've agreed to meet with a friend over lunch.

To exit yourself from a conversation, have a 'conversation ender' prepared. For example:

'I've really enjoyed talking to you, and I'm pleased to have met you. I'm guessing we have both come here to mix and meet people, and I don't want to monopolise you and stop you from meeting other people. Is there anyone here you want to meet? Perhaps I, or one of our hosts, can make the introduction for you?'

Breaking into a group

Everyone at a networking event is looking to meet people. So, logically, most people will be very welcoming if you come up and ask to speak to them. However, there is an art form to breaking into groups and conversations.

> **❝There is an art form to breaking into groups and conversations❞**

A room full of people is never static – conversations are always starting and ending, and people recirculating. The way to spot whether a conversation is private or public is to look at how the group is standing. Any group that has an open side and people looking out from the group is likely to be happy to be joined by more people (see Figure 10.1). Any group where all the members are looking into the group and are effectively closed probably is having a private conversation and doesn't want to be disturbed (see Figure 10.2).

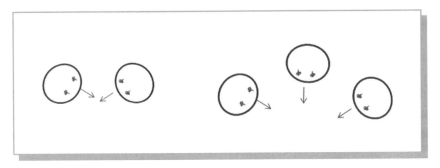

figure 10.1   An open pair and group

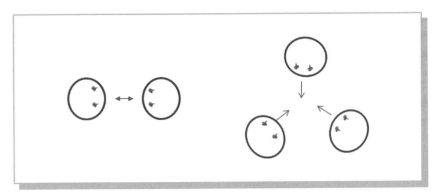

figure 10.2   A closed pair and group

When looking for a new group of people to join, always look for someone standing on their own, or an open pair or group.

Don't just assume that a group of people will want you to join their conversation. As you approach the group, make eye contact and smile. Then ask the group,

'Is it OK if I join in?'

If the answer is 'No', don't take the rejection personally – their conversation probably was a private one.

However, there are times when you want to speak to someone in a closed group. A great tactic is to position yourself so you can see the group and wait until it changes formation, from closed to open. This is a sign that the conversation is losing its intensity and members of the group want to recirculate, and it is appropriate for you to ask to join in the conversation.

If the group shows no sign of changing formation, then hover around near the group and make eye contact with a member of the group – they are likely to ask you to join them.

As a last resort, if there is someone in the closed group you really want to speak to, approach the group, apologise for interrupting them and say you will take up only 30 seconds of their time. State that you would like to speak to Mr 'X' after they have finished their conversation, perhaps over lunch, and then depart from the group.

Changing a group's dynamic

If you find yourself in a closed group and want to change the dynamics of the conversation, position your body so that you are looking out of the group and make eye contact with people who are circulating near the group. This will encourage other people to join your group and naturally change the dynamic of the conversation.

Business card etiquette

When you hand over your business card, you are giving permission to be contacted by the other person (you are not giving permission to go on to their mailing list!). Some people when networking literally go business card hunting and gathering. There is no benefit to coming back from an event with more than 100 business cards if you haven't taken the time to build a relationship with the other person. All this does is help increase a printer's business.

If you have enjoyed meeting someone and want to stay in touch with them, then ask them for their business card. For example:

'I've enjoyed talking to you today and would like to stay in touch with you. Can we swap business cards?'

Most people, when asked for their business card, naturally will provide it and ask for yours in return. Don't make the mistake of asking for someone's business card at the start of the conversation, as this gives the impression that you are just wanting to grab their contact details for a mailing list.

After you have met someone, use their business card to jot down some notes about them. Before you write on someone's business card, check that it is acceptable to do so. In some cultures, for example China, it is considered rude to write on someone else's business card.

Tip

Write down on a person's business card if they are happy to be signed up to your mailing list and connect with you on LinkedIn and/or Twitter.

❝The notes that you make at the time of meeting may be invaluable❞

A week after a networking event, where you may have met up to 30 people, it's very hard to recall every single person or conversation that you had. The notes that you make at the time of meeting may be invaluable for personalising future communications with them. Here are some ideas for what you can write down about them:

- What they were wearing (if particularly memorable).
- Personal details about them – children? hobbies? mutual connections?
- Details about their company.

The contents of your networker's toolkit

Every networker should carry the following items:

- Multiple copies of their business card.
- Good quality biro and small notepad.
- Name badge.

Your business card

A business card is still business's preferred way of exchanging contact details when meeting someone face-to-face. I suspect in the next 10 years that physical business cards may be phased out in favour of virtual business cards, but, until then, we are stuck with actual physical business cards. Most companies will provide their client-facing employees with a business card. If you don't have your own card, or you want a business card that is not branded with your employer's contact details, then get your own made up.

> **Tips**
>
> Print on both sides of your business card, but leave some white space for people to write on your card.
>
> Don't choose a glossy or laminate finish for your business card. They may look impressive but are very hard for people to write on.

What needs to go on your business card (see Figure 10.3)?

■ Your name.

■ Your company name (if appropriate).

■ Your job title (if appropriate).

■ A mailing address – normally now you need include only your email address rather than your physical address.

■ Phone numbers – preferably a direct line where you can always be reached.

■ Your company logo.

■ You may choose to put your services and products on the back of your card, or some 'valuable' information (as shown in Figure 10.3).

Good quality biro and small notepad

You may be thinking, why a biro? Many people's business cards are laminated, and anything written using a wet ink, such as a fountain pen, easily rubs off on your hand... other business cards... your shirt pocket... the inside of your handbag.

Make sure that you use a high-quality biro. A chewed-up, 'been-around-the-block' biro is not going to leave people with the professional image you have been trying to carefully craft. There is also nothing worse than greeting people with ink-stained hands!

There are many ways that you can capture information for what you have agreed to do for a new contact – for example on their business card, or on your mini networking notepad. This notepad needs to be the size of a cigarette packet and fit easily into your handbag or your suit pocket.

Writing down what you've committed to do with your new contact shows that you are serious about developing a good quality relationship with your new contact. Most people will be very happy for you to say, 'If you don't mind, I'll just write that down so I don't forget'. Then, grab your notepad and quickly capture what you have just agreed to do.

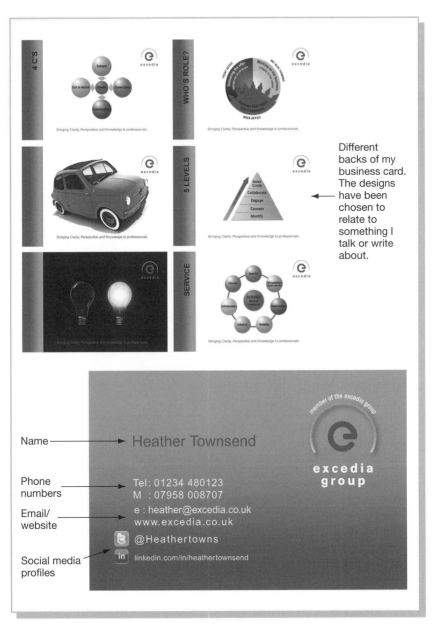

Different backs of my business card. The designs have been chosen to relate to something I talk or write about.

Name → Heather Townsend

Phone numbers → Tel: 01234 480123
M : 07958 008707

Email/ website → e : heather@excedia.co.uk
www.excedia.co.uk

Social media profiles → @Heathertowns
linkedin.com/in/heathertownsend

figure 10.3 Details for your business card

Source: A.N.G. Creative Design

Name badge

❝Make sure your name is in large lettering that people can read❞

A personalised name badge looks professional and makes sure that you always have a correctly spelled name badge, regardless of how well organised the event is. Make sure your name is in large lettering that people can read without needing to reach for their glasses.

> **Tip**
>
> Choose a badge with a magnetic fastening, as these badges can be used on any outfit without damaging the fabric.

Making the most of your one-to-one meetings

Many people you meet when networking will suggest that the two of you get together for a longer conversation – in networking circles often called 'a one-to-one'. If you are not sure whether you would benefit from a face-to-face meeting, then arrange a phone conversation first to get to know them better.

> **Tip**
>
> If you have a lot of people you want to have a meeting with, then block out a day in your diary. Locate yourself in a hotel lounge and arrange as many of these meetings as you can for that day in the hotel lounge.

The aim of any one-to-one meeting is to strengthen the relationship. However, many people will have an agenda for this meeting. It may be to sell you something, or they are interested in buying your services. Early into a one-to-one meeting, remember to ask the other person:

'What are you looking to achieve in this meeting?'

If the conversation has gone well, towards the end of the meeting, ask:

'How can we help each other?' and *'Who do you know who would benefit from my services?'*

Summary

The skills needed for working a room can be learned, and may need to be practised if you are a shy person.

If you are targeting a specific person, contact them beforehand and arrange to meet them at the event.

Once you realise that a conversation is unproductive for you, work out a way to break off without offending the other person. If you meet an A-lister, then ask for a further one-to-one conversation.

Look to join open groups of people or individuals on their own.

If you want to stay in touch with someone, ask for their business card and suggest that you contact them in the coming weeks.

ACTION POINTS

▦ When next you are looking for someone to talk to at a business or social gathering, have a go at making eye contact and smiling at someone you would like to speak to.

▦ At your next face-to-face networking event, look for pairs and open groups to break into conversation with.

▦ When standing talking with people, aim to keep the circle closed for the first five minutes so you can focus on the other person. Then open up a gap to allow others to join you.

▦ When talking with people in a group, check to see whether everyone is interested and contributing to the conversation. Invite the quieter members of the group to contribute to the discussion.

▦ If you don't have a business card, get one made up with your contact details on.

▦ Next time you attend a face-to-face networking event, arrange to meet someone at the event.

▦ If you go networking with a colleague, agree to split up and each work a different side of the room. At the end of the event compare notes.

▦ Get an attendance list in advance of the event you are attending and divide up targets between all the people attending the event from your company. Agree in advance with the people attending from your company when you will reconvene and share information.

▦ Have a go at attending a networking event on your own.

▦ Next time you are out networking, write some details about each person you meet on their business card. Remember to capture these details on your client relationship management system.

Further resources

Books

D'Souza, S., *Brilliant Networking: What the best networkers know, do and say*, 2nd edition, Prentice Hall, 2010.

Frankel, L.P., *Nice Girls Don't Get the Corner Office*, Little, Brown & Company, 2004.

Lindenfield, G. and Lindenfield, S., *Confident Networking for Career Success and Satisfaction*, Piatkus Books, 2010.

Misner, I.R., Alexander, D.C. and Hilliard, B., *Networking Like a Pro: Turning contacts into connections*, Entrepreneur Press, 2010.

Blogs and websites

Joined Up Networking www.joinedupnetworking.com

Winning business – the secrets of working a room www.winningbusiness.net/downloads/pdfs/WorkingRoom.pdf

11

How to ask for referrals and introductions

What topics are covered in this chapter?

- What is meant by a referral
- How people like to give referrals
- The right way to ask for a referral
- The best time to ask for a referral
- How to become more referable

In the last chapter we gave you the skills to flourish in a crowded room. In this chapter we will show you how to ask for referrals and introductions effortlessly, regardless of whom you are with. These skills could help you find your next job or win new business.

What is meant by a referral?

Spend any time in the company of networkers or professionals and you will hear the word 'referral' being bandied around. These people talk about referrals as if they are the Holy Grail. In fact, many business networking groups are structured around the concept of passing referrals to each other. But, what exactly is a referral? How does this differ from a recommendation, a lead or a warm prospect?

- *A recommendation:* This is where someone will recommend your services to others. In fact, they may even go as far as giving you a glowing recommendation when they share your contact details.

A recommendation often will give you a warm prospect. However, at this point there is no guarantee that the person will contact you.

■ *An introduction:* This is where you are introduced to someone. There may be no recommendation or referral involved in the introduction.

■ *A warm prospect:* A prospect, unlike a lead, has not yet proactively asked to use your services, buy your products or consider you for a job vacancy. However, with the information you know about them and the prior conversations you have had, there is a strong possibility that the prospect will turn into a lead.

■ *A lead:* This is when someone has asked proactively to use your services, buy your products or consider you for a vacancy.

■ *A referral:* This is like a recommendation on steroids. It is where the person who is referring you gives you a glowing recommendation, and actively makes sure that you and the person who needs your services have a conversation. A good referral almost always results in you generating a lead.

❝A recommendation gives you a warm fuzzy feeling, but not much else❞

As Andy Lopata states in his book, *Recommended: How to sell through networking and referrals*, many people wrongly confuse a recommendation with a referral.[1] Whilst it is lovely to get recommended, unless the person to whom you have been recommended gets in contact with you, a recommendation gives you a warm fuzzy feeling, but not much else.

How people like to give referrals

Standard networking theory touted by most networking gurus goes like this:

'If you want to generate more referrals for your business or find a new job, ask people you meet, "Who do you know who needs…?"'

Whilst this advice may work if you are doing your 60-second or networker's pitch, generally it doesn't work at all outside of this very formal networking group environment. If you are like me and you have tried it, at best it leads to a couple of hastily identified recommendations, which rarely go any-

---

[1] Lopata, A., *Recommended: How to sell through networking and referrals*, FT Prentice Hall, 2011.

where. In fact, for many years, I thought it was just me who wasn't able to get any leads when I asked this question of the people I met whilst out networking.

Here are the reasons why this approach rarely works:

1   People like to give referrals when they spot an opportunity for someone they like in their network. They do this for reasons such as social recognition, generating social capital, problem solving, visibility or just because they enjoy helping out people. The trigger for the referral to take place is spotting the opportunity, not being asked for a referral.

2   When you ask someone for a referral, it puts them on the spot. As a result, they don't get the valuable thinking time needed to answer this question to a higher standard.

3   If you haven't established your credibility or relationship before you ask for the referral, the other person may not want to damage their own credibility by recommending you to others.

The right way to ask for a referral

Therefore, if the advice to ask people 'Who do you know...' rarely leads to a decent referral, then how do you ask correctly for a referral or introduction? Very simply, you want to ask for help and advice, not for the referral. Let me illustrate this:

Instead of asking,

'Who do you know who needs the services of an accountant?'

say,

'I wonder whether I could ask for some advice? I'm keen to find some new clients for my accountancy practice. The kind of clients we are looking for are, typically, IT contractors. If you were in my position, what would you do to find these clients?'

or,

'I'd love to speak to the finance director at your company. If you were in my position, what would be the best way to get a meeting fixed up with them?'

Instead of asking,

'I'm looking for a new job, who do you know who is hiring IT contractors at the moment?'

say,

'Would it be OK to ask you for some help? I'm now thinking about where my next IT contract will come from. I know you are pretty well connected to the IT community locally. What local companies have you heard about who are about to start up a new IT project?'

You then spend time with them exploring the help or advice that they are giving to you. At some point in the conversation, they may remember someone who would be an ideal introduction, employer or referral for you. Typically, most people then will offer to make the introduction or referral, there and then.

The best time to ask for a referral

Ivan Misner, founder of BNI, uses a term called 'premature solicitation' to describe the moment of exquisite social discomfort, when someone you barely know asks you for an introduction or referral. Many an eager networker, or job hunter, has come unstuck by asking someone too early into their relationship for a referral or introduction. In fact, premature solicitation can kill a relationship before it really has got going.

If you remember, in Chapter 3, I talked about the requirement to have built up credibility and social capital before someone will recommend you to others. Therefore, the best time to ask for a referral or introduction is when someone is saying positive things about you. This could be because you have just done a great job for them or helped them out in some way. For example:

'I'm really pleased that you are highly delighted with the results we have achieved together. May I be cheeky and ask a favour of you? How well do you know your opposite number in your firm's Manchester office? If you were in my position, how would you go about checking that they could also benefit from working with me?'

'I really appreciate your offer of helping me out by introducing me to people in your network. My ideal client is one who is a micro business owner, local and over 50. What would you recommend I do in order to meet more of these types of people?'

As an aside, if you do find yourself on the wrong side of a corporate restructuring, this is one of the very few times when you can be fairly direct with your requests for introductions to people within your soon-to-be ex-employers. Having been through this situation twice, I know that the people who are staying often feel incredibly guilty that they got to keep their job, whilst you didn't. As a consequence they, if they think it will help you get another job, are often exceptionally helpful with introductions, recommendations and general information sharing.

How to become more referable

Having a network is one thing, but using it to generate referrals or opportunities reliably week in, week out, is quite another thing. Your personal networking strategy, which we will help you build in Part 4, will get you talking to, and in front of, the right people, but, if you don't say the right things, then you will miss out on opportunities to generate referrals via your network.

The SERVICE referral framework (see Figure 11.1) will help you use your networking activities to maximise the number of referrals you get through your network. SERVICE stands for:

Specific

Extraordinary client service

Relationships

Visibility

Initiative

Collaborate

Educate

Specific

❝You can't be all things to all people❞

In Chapter 2 we talked about the importance of your personal brand. In order to be memorable in your network, you can't be all things to all people. You need to commit to marketing to a niche or specialist skill set.

Being specific is more than just being committed to your niche. It is also about being specific with your requests about who you want to be introduced to.

Extraordinary client service

A good friend of mine, Simone, a project director for the manufacturing sector, finds that every new client comes to her pretty much pre-sold on the

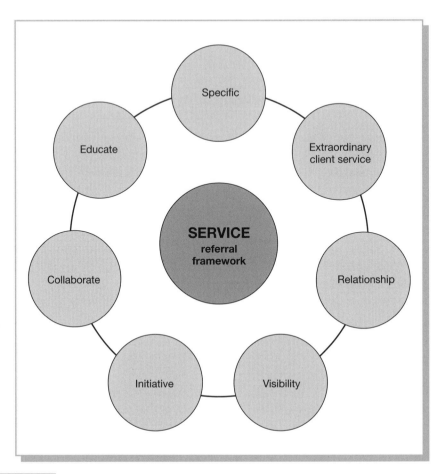

figure 11.1   The SERVICE referral framework

basis of multiple personal recommendations. However, you will only get this word-of-mouth business if you deliver to clients not just good service, but extraordinary service – the type of client service that just compels your clients to tell others about it. (Warning, if you don't deliver on the basics of client service then any attempt to deliver extraordinary client service will be wasted effort.) Luckily, extraordinary client service can be delivered easily fairly cheaply with just a little thought about what will make the difference to your clients. For example, how about:

■ Keeping a stock of mobile phone rechargers in your office for when clients visit, so that they can charge their phone whilst they meet with you or your team.

- Taking note of your client's dietary preferences, so that you can always offer them a hot beverage and something to eat that you know they can eat/drink and enjoy.

- Having some umbrellas in the office so you can walk clients out to their cars when it is raining.

- Sending them birthday cards.

- Introducing them to one potential client or referrer every six months.

- Sending them a small gift, relevant to the work you are doing, after your work is completed. For example a conveyancing solicitor sending a small food hamper to their clients on completion day.

Relationships

As already covered, in Chapter 7, a small core of relationships, i.e. your A-listers, will result in a large proportion of your referrals and beneficial introductions. In Part 4 you will be encouraged to write and implement relationship plans to stay close to these A-listers and maximise the benefits of your relationship with them.

Visibility

Being seen in all the right places, whether online or offline, is a major component for referral generation. For example, Aakar, when he was building his reputation as the go-to lawyer for the pharmaceutical industry, made sure he was present physically at all the big pharmaceutical trade shows. Your personal networking strategy (see Part 4) will make sure that you are networking and being seen in all the right places.

Initiative

❝Ask proactively for referrals and introductions❞ Many of my clients moan to me that their people never proactively ask for referrals. Often people don't ask for referrals because either they feel uncomfortable doing so, or they don't know how. One of the best ways of getting the help you require from your network, whether it is an introduction to a potential employer or client, is to ask proactively for referrals and introductions. (See earlier in this chapter for the best way to do this.)

When clients or people in your network give you referrals or introductions, ask their permission to use their name when making contact. Or even suggest that you could prepare an introduction for them to use via the phone or email.

Collaborate

Working together with other professionals who share the same market as you can be one of the most powerful ways to generate referrals. Who do you know who has a similar type of client base to you, but offers a different service? In the early days of your relationship, you may want to help each other out with little things, such as:

- writing blog posts for each other
- quoting them in an article
- recommending them in your newsletters.

As the relationship, trust and credibility builds, it's worth thinking about bigger things you can do together, such as:

- launching a joint service or product
- running a marketing event or campaign together
- systematically introducing all your new clients to them, with an easy incentive to use their services.

---

case study   The Franchise Surgery

The Franchise Surgery is a series of surgeries for existing franchisors to come in and speak to professional advisors who specialise in franchising. The surgery was co-founded by Carl Reader, an accountant who specialises in franchising. For each surgery, they tend to get 6–10 franchisors. Every professional advisor in attendance normally comes away with invoiceable business from each surgery session.

Educate

If you want your network to act as an unpaid sales force for you, then you will need to educate them on how to spot a potential client, how much you value them doing this for you, and what to do next. How can your network physically see, hear, taste or even smell that someone needs your services? What are the sorts of comments that you will hear them say?

For example, someone who may be ready to change their accountant will say things like:

'I'm not sure what my accountant actually does to justify what he is charging me.'

'My accountant only seems to get in touch with me when he wants his bill paid or year-end is upon us.'

'I'm unhappy with the current level of service I am receiving from my accountant.'

'My business is growing rapidly and I think it may be outgrowing my current accountant.'

You also need to educate your network that giving you referrals is a good thing. Do this by saying thank you. You could:

■ Send them a handwritten note saying thank you.

■ Give them a gift.

■ Give them a referral in return.

■ Buy them lunch or a drink.

■ Offer them a spotter's fee or commission split for any successful introductions or referrals. Be aware that some professionals may not be able to accept a spotter's fee or commission split, either for ethical or regulatory reasons.

Summary

The best way to ask for referrals is not to ask directly for a referral or introduction, but to ask for advice on how to achieve your networking objectives.

To help make yourself more referable, think SERVICE, i.e.

Specific: commit to a memorable personal brand, in particular a niche marketplace or specialist skill set.

Extraordinary client service: keep your credibility high by delivering extraordinary client service.

Relationships: focus your networking time on the 10 per cent of your network who will be able to help you achieve 90 per cent of your career or business goals, i.e. your A-listers.

Visibility: use relationship plans to make sure that you achieve top-of-mind visibility with your A-listers.

Initiative: remember to ask proactively for referrals and introductions from your network.

Collaborate: who can you work together with to help each other?

Educate: help your network learn who would make a great client for you, and what to do if they spot someone like this.

ACTION POINTS

■ Next time a client says positive things about you, ask them for an introduction to someone who could be a good prospect for you.

■ Look through your network, and identify two people with whom you could collaborate for quick mutual gain. Now take action and talk to these two people about collaborating.

■ Next time someone makes a good introduction or referral for you, do something to thank them formally.

■ Look through your client list and identify your top 10 clients. Who in your network would these clients love to meet? Now commit to making one beneficial introduction a month for each of these top 10 clients.

Further resources

Books

Lopata, A., *Recommended: How to sell through networking and referrals*, FT Prentice Hall, 2011.

Misner, I.R., Alexander, D.C. and Hilliard, B., *Networking Like a Pro: Turning contacts into connections*, Entrepreneur Press, 2010.

Townsend, H. and Baker, J., *The Go-To Expert: How to build your reputation, differentiate yourself from the competition, and win business*, FT Publishing, 2014.

Blogs and websites

Business Networking www.business-networking.co.uk

Joined Up Networking www.joinedupnetworking.com

Relationology – the art and science of creating relationships www.relationology.co.uk

12

How to build your own community

What topics are covered in this chapter?

■ The personal benefits of building your own community

■ The seven steps needed to create a successful and active community

In the last five chapters we have explored the skills professionals need to develop successful relationships through online and offline networking. In this chapter we will explore both 'why' you should consider developing a community from your network and 'how' to do this.

What is a community?

An active community is one where people meet and interact. Before social media burst on to the scene, this used to be limited to groups who met face-to-face, united by a common goal, interest or purpose. For example, a local residents' association, a football supporters' club, an amateur dramatics society or a professional association.

Online communities, such as a LinkedIn group, Facebook group, fan or business page, are still built around common interests, but the exchange of ideas can happen 24 hours per day, and may extend across geographic borders.

Examples of communities I have created or joined:

■ My large Twitter following (11,000 at the time of writing).

■ The Professional Speaking Association UK and Ireland's Facebook Group (6,000+ members at the time of writing), which is open to anyone, not just members, who want to improve their speaking and build their speaking business.

■ The Authors and Marketing Google+ community, where fellow authors discuss how to market our books.

Why build your own community?

Having your own community puts you at the centre of your network. Imagine what it would be like if you could bring all your A-listers together in one place – especially if it is a place where you are seen to be at the centre of all worthwhile conversations.

When you have your own community, you become the main conduit or concierge to this community. Some professions, such as accountants and business coaches, naturally become concierges to their networks of clients. Think how powerful it would be to create a community out of this network – and how much value you could add back to your clients by introducing them all to each other.

As a concierge to your community, you can attract additional opportunities. For example, Sharon Gaskin (founder of The Trainers Training Company) has built a community of over 4,000+ trainers via LinkedIn.[1] Her aim is to help trainers grow successful businesses, so she focuses her networking efforts on meeting freelance or newly freelancing trainers. Sharon benefits in three ways from her LinkedIn community. First, she enjoys having active contact with 4,000+ passionate trainers. Second, she is the hub, so she has a position that oversees everything that is happening. But, most importantly, she is the focal point through which opportunities flow to the entire group.

Why do people join a community?

Humans have a need to belong and connect with others. People will join a community because they have had an experience, want to find some answers, to meet like-minded people or to be identified with a certain

---

[1] www.thetrainerstrainingcompany.co.uk

❝Humans have a need to belong and connect with others❞

community. For example, I became active with the local branch of the Chartered Institute of Personnel and Development because it enhanced my credibility as a learning and development specialist, but also increased my profile with potential local buyers of my services.

Whilst people enjoy the feeling of belonging to a community, not everyone has the desire to contribute content or time to one. Very often only a few community members will want to be involved actively in the discussions or the running of an event. Josh Bernoff and Charlene Li, in their book *Groundswell*, identified the 90-9-1 rule for online communities: 90 per cent of your population will browse or lurk, 9 per cent will comment or engage and 1 per cent will create content.[2]

Why people don't join or participate in an online community

There are many reasons why online communities are full of lurkers. First, there are millions of social networking sites available; most people don't have the time or inclination to contribute to every site. Some social networking sites can be very cliquey and often can be the online equivalent of entering a pub and feeling as if everyone has turned around and wondered why you have come in.

Steps to build your own community

1 What's the purpose of your community?

Beginning with your personal goals, decide on why you want to build your own community and what benefits it will bring the potential members. Starting a community because you want to keep close to your network is, perhaps, a good reason, but not a powerful enough reason to attract members. What's in it for the people who join your community?

Be aware that what the community wants and actually does will evolve over time, which in the long term may not help you achieve your personal goals.

---

[2] Bernoff, J. and Li, C., *Groundswell*, Harvard Business School Press, expanded and revised edn, 2011.

'There has to be a shared interest or topic which will bring people to your community – your sparkling personality is not enough.'

Mariam Cook, digital engagement expert[3]

2 Identify and find your members

Who is your ideal community member? Is it a potential client or, perhaps, existing clients, or both? Will you keep the membership of your community closed and by exclusive invitation only? Or will you let it be open to all?

---

case study   The Professional Speaking Association UK and Ireland (PSAUKI) Facebook Group

At the time of writing the group has over 6,000 members, not all of whom are members of the PSAUKI. The group is a place to share resources and ask questions that are helpful and related to the speaking business. Over a 12-month period, the group size grew by a factor of 10, and was a key driver in the PSAUKI doubling its membership.

The group's success is due to a mixture of high-quality information being shared, coupled with very heavy moderation that does not allow any promotion or self-promotion by the members of the group.

You will need to be proactive to find the right members for your community. Unless you have celebrity status, don't expect that people will join magically as soon as you switch the group on. Having the right kind of early members, e.g. proactive advocates, in your community is vital for the success of your future community. Your early members need to be in the 10 per cent of people who will create content and comment on content. Remember the principle of social proof – people will want to join and actively participate if people like them are already present and contributing.

When you invite your first few members, include in the invitation how they will personally benefit from joining the community – and how personally they can help grow a vibrant community.

3 Create visible guidelines for your community

Unless you educate your community about what is and what isn't acceptable behaviour, you risk building an online community with poor-quality

---

[3] http://uk.linkedin.com/pub/mariam-cook/5/224/a8a

content and low-value conversations. For example, will you allow people to post content that blatantly advertises their services? Will you specify criteria that potential members need to satisfy before they can join? Many companies aim to stay in contact with their alumni, for instance. Unsurprisingly, entry to these companies' alumni communities is dependent on whether you have worked for them.

> **Not everyone is a clear-cut spammer**

Make sure you display prominently these guidelines and stick to them. I can promise you that you will have to deal with people transgressing the rules of your community. Sadly, I have to purge my Facebook groups and Twitter followers regularly of spammers who want to entice me to click through to a porn site. But not everyone is a clear-cut spammer. For example, what about the recruiter, even though it is against the rules of your community, who occasionally posts about a job vacancy? Or the blogger who posts up a blog that is a thinly veiled advert for their products? Or the member in your networking group who keeps on selling to people? Have you thought about how you are going to moderate your community and manage unacceptable behaviour? One strike and you are out, or a friendly warning first?

4 Where will you host your community?

'Unless you have enough spare time and resources to build a social website from scratch, first think about using a 'plug in and go' solution to host your community.'

Mariam Cook, digital engagement expert

Your members will need a place to meet – whether face-to-face or online. For your online network, will you use a groups feature on a big social networking site, such as LinkedIn's Groups[4] feature, a Google+ community[5], a Yahoo Group, or set up your own Facebook Group or business page?[6] Or is the right 'venue' your own fully customisable social network, such as Ning?[7]

5 Fine-tune and seed content before going public

A community is a living organism. Unless it has died, it is never static, and the dynamics of the community will change over time. Personally invite

[4] www.linkedin.com/directory/groups
[5] www.google.com/+/learnmore/communities/
[6] www.facebook.com/pages/create.php?
[7] www.ning.com

your first handful of members and ask them to seed content and proactively comment on posts and discussions. Once you have some content within your site, consider making the community public. No one likes joining the online equivalent of a ghost town.

6 Maintaining momentum

An active group, regardless of whether it meets face-to-face or online, which has a genuine sense of community, will attract more like-minded individuals. The principle of social proof tells us that people like to be identified with successful communities. This means that your aim as the founder of the community is to get to the point where members invite their friends and network to join because it is a great place to hang out.

To create the environment where your members invite others to join, think about regularly doing the following:

■ Spend time encouraging and rewarding contribution. How can you generate status for members of your community who contribute to the success of the community?

■ Include an area within the online forum or a mechanism for face-to-face groups where new members can introduce themselves and start to engage with the group.

■ Make it easy for people to join the conversation, such as asking questions that invite a response.

■ Ask for feedback from the community on how the community could be improved for the members.

■ Run face-to-face or online events for the community.

■ Welcome criticism and healthy debate – but respond positively to any negative comments.

■ Have regular communications with the members of the community, e.g. newsletters or broadcasts.

As the community grows, it becomes harder to run and moderate it by yourself. Create a management team with defined roles and responsibilities within the community to spread the load. This management team could be regional champions, moderators or the more traditional face-to-face community leadership structure, e.g. chairperson, treasurer, membership advisor, secretary, fundraiser/events organiser.

7 Promote your community

> **Where do potential members of your community hang out?**

Unless you want your community to be one of the best-kept secrets, you will need still to promote it. How can you automate the process of finding new members for the community? Where can you talk about it? Where do potential members of your community hang out?

Different ways in which you can promote your community include:

- advertising on your business card
- advertising on your email signature
- writing about your community in your newsletters and mail shots
- writing something on your LinkedIn, Google+, Twitter or Facebook status updates
- a mention within other communities of which you are a member
- a tweet about the community.

Summary

Building your own community takes a lot of effort on your part, but the reward is professional credibility.

The seven steps to building and maintaining a community are:

1 Deciding on the purpose of the community.

2 Identifying and finding your members.

3 Creating guidelines for membership.

4 Deciding where you will meet.

5 Fine-tuning and seeding content before publicly launching your community.

6 Maintaining momentum and interaction.

7 Promoting your community.

> **ACTION POINTS**
>
> ■ What do your A-listers like to talk about and discuss? How could you set up an online community to meet that need? What would be your membership criteria and rules of the group?
>
> ■ What clubs or societies would your A-listers already belong to and would you enjoy being a member of? How could you play an active part within the club?
>
> ■ How could you build a community with influential people within your company?
>
> ■ Volunteer to be a moderator for one of the online communities in which you regularly participate.
>
> ■ If you already run an online community, think of three ways in which you can encourage more participation within your community.
>
> ■ What group, such as a mastermind group, could you set up to strengthen your networking with your A-listers?

Further resources

Books

Bernoff, J. and Li, C., *Groundswell*, expanded and revised edition, Harvard Business School Press, 2011.

Gladwell, M., *The Tipping Point*, Abacus, 2001.

O'Keefe, P., *Managing Online Forums*, Amacom, 2008.

Online community hosting

Facebook groups www.facebook.com/groups

Facebook business and community pages www.facebook.com/pages/create.php?

Ning www.ning.com

Google+ Communities www.google.com/+/learnmore/communities/

LinkedIn groups www.linkedin.com/directory/groups

Yahoo groups https://uk.groups.yahoo.com

13

International networking

What topics are covered in this chapter?

- How to use online networking to break down cultural differences
- How to fit in and relate to people, regardless of the cultural, geographical and social differences between you
- When it is appropriate and expected to show emotion
- What is the appropriate greeting for a stranger in different cultures
- How to adapt your language when talking with non-native speakers
- How to change your discussion style, depending on the culture you are in
- When and how to exchange business cards

'As global virtual teams become increasingly prevalent, a successful professional has to find ways to work across organisational, cultural, functional and geographical boundaries.'

Hamish Taylor, Shinergise Partners Ltd

The media has been telling us incorrectly for many years that the world is getting smaller. It's actually the rapid advancement in communications technology that has made the world feel smaller. Twenty-five years ago letters taking weeks to arrive were the norm for international communications, expensive international phone calls were saved for special occasions and email was very much in its infancy. Fast forward to today, and many people don't think twice about sending an email across to the other side of the world, or making a free or cheap international video call to foreign climes. Email and the internet have enabled international communication to happen simply, rapidly and cheaply. Even though international communication is now as easy as making a local phone call, cultural differences persist – and will persist for the foreseeable future. Today's networker, to succeed in the global marketplace, now more than ever, has to be aware of the cultural differences that exist. In this chapter we will look at the skills and awareness that a networker needs to build successful relationships internationally, regardless of what national culture they are working in or across.

Online networking as an enabler

'We look at how they dress, we look at the houses that they live in, and the cars they drive and then we label people.'

Sharon Carville, HR professional

Our brains are programmed to make assumptions based on material possessions, appearances and how a person speaks. They do this because, historically, our very survival rested on how quickly we made a judgement on whether they were friend or foe. As we found out in Chapter 10, the more shared common interests, the more likely that rapport and a relationship will develop between two people. Online communication tends to be solely by the written word. This means that cultural differences that are emphasised often by appearances, material possessions, body language and verbal language are, very often, not apparent. This means we may also miss the visual and audible clues that might cause us to approach a person in a different manner, so it is worth spending longer building up a relationship online before moving to a face-to-face or telephone meeting.

> **Online communication tends to be solely by the written word**

Observe and adapt

'There are more differences between people than there are between cultures. These are mostly behavioural style differences rather than necessarily cultural differences.'

Ivan Misner, founder of BNI

People within a distinct culture have different beliefs, attitudes and ways of doing things. Everyone is slightly different – no two people are actually

100 per cent alike in both mind and body. You see these microcosms of culture also happening within a business. Different teams, departments and offices within a single business will all have slightly different cultures or, more simply, different 'ways of thinking and doing'. The organisation may be bound together tightly by commonly held values and beliefs, but not everyone will interpret or act on these in the same way. A floor with an open-plan office will have a different feel and vibe to a floor within the same building, where some individuals have their own offices.

Successful networkers are aware of potential differences between people and behaviours – and are continually on the lookout for signs to give them clues about what are acceptable behaviours, and what are not. Expertly networking across different cultures is more than just being able to rapidly adjust and conform to expected behaviour. Your research before travelling or meeting anyone from a different background to yourself will give you clues to watch out for and what to expect. For example, what is the appropriate greeting for a stranger and a friend? When is it OK to shake a woman's hand? How should you exchange business cards? What's the typical style for a discussion? Does a meeting timetabled for 15:00 really mean it will start at 15:00?

As the saying goes, when in Rome, do as the Romans do.

Expressive versus reserved cultures

There are lots of examples where we see cultural stereotypes being used, especially in comedy. The British are always portrayed as being reserved. Some of the southern European cultures are shown as being very loud and waving their arms around when they talk. Some Asian cultures are depicted as ultra-polite. Whilst we have to be careful not to label people we meet automatically, it is helpful to at least be on the lookout for behaviours in business people that are different from our own. If you are talking with someone from an expressive culture, for example an Italian, you would expect more *feel*-type communication, whereas with someone from a reserved culture, such as Japan, you would see more *know* and *think* types of communication. To increase your ability to relate and connect with someone from a different cultural background to you, listen out for the amount of *feel*-type communication and adapt the amount of emotion and feeling you display to match their level.

The websites Executive Planet (www.executiveplanet.com), Kwintessential (www.kwintessential.co.uk/resources/country-profiles.html) and Cyborlink (www.cyborlink.com) have some guidelines that you should read prior to meeting with people from other countries.

Reserved	Expressive
UK	Southern Europe
Japan	Middle East
Northern Europe	Egypt
Ethiopia	Russia
China	South America

Unsurprisingly, the degree of expressiveness within a culture heavily influences people's preference for one of the three communication styles – *think*, *feel* or *know*.

Communication style	Preference
Think	UK, Japan
Feel	Southern Europe
Know	Scandinavia, Germany, Austria

Appropriate greetings

From the formal British handshake to the reserved Japanese bow to the French spontaneous kiss on both cheeks, greeting people – whether a stranger or a good friend – varies across different cultures. The more expressive a culture, the more likely the greeting will involve closeness of physical contact. The greeting of a kiss on both cheeks favoured by the expressive Mediterranean cultures requires both parties to fully enter each other's personal space, whereas a handshake, the preferred greeting used by the reserved British and Americans, requires far less invasion of each other's personal space.

> **Tip**
>
> If you are in a situation where you are wondering what an appropriate greeting is, follow the example given by others around you.

It is worth noting that some religions, for example Islam, forbid physical contact between unmarried or non-related men and women. As a rule of thumb, if a religion requires women to cover their face or hair, then there is a strong likelihood that a handshake – or any physical contact with a man to whom a woman is not related – is deemed inappropriate behaviour.

Language and the spoken word

'I find one of the most effective opening questions to be "How's it going?" in whatever the local informal style of asking is, e.g. "Do desu-ka?" is Japanese for "How is it?"'

Hamish Taylor, Shinergise Partners

English may be the predominant language used in international business, but a trip to the USA, or even places in the UK with a strong regional dialect and accent, such as the North East, will demonstrate that the English language is used very differently in different geographical locations. When you are communicating with non-native English speakers, eliminate any slang or colloquialisms, as these may lead to misunderstandings.

For example, instead of saying

'Give me a bell.'

or

'Drop me a line.'

say

'Let's arrange a time for a telephone call.'

or

'Please send me an email.'

When someone is communicating in a language with which they are not fully familiar, they will have a tendency to say 'Yes' to any question – even if they do not fully understand the question. Therefore, use open-ended questions or phrases that test their understanding, e.g.

'Please summarise your understanding for me.'

rather than

'Can you tell me what you need to do?'

Different cultures have different styles of discussions. In Anglo-Saxon cultures, silence is seen to be uncomfortable, and someone will start talking when someone else finishes speaking. Interrupting someone before they have finished talking is seen to be rude. Yet the Latin temperaments happily

> ❝In Anglo-Saxon cultures, silence is seen to be uncomfortable❞

will tolerate a small amount of interruption, as this is seen to be a sign of interest in the subject, rather than rudeness. The Oriental cultures like to have time to reflect on and digest what has been said, as this shows respect for the person who has been talking. Therefore, when you are talking with someone from China, expect silences in a discussion and any interruptions in conversation will be seen as disrespectful.

Tip

Whenever you are attempting to speak a little in a foreign language, always smile – as this will make you seem more welcoming and help break the ice.

When you need to engage cross-culturally, take the time to learn the basics of 'Please', 'Thank you', 'Yes', 'No', 'Good morning', etc. If you find that you are a regular visitor to a country where you are not a native speaker of the language, take the time to learn a little more of the language, for example 'No problem' in that language. When Hamish Taylor, partner at Shinergise, is running workshops in different countries, he finds that using a few words of the delegates' native language builds engagement and helps to create connectivity between people.

Business cards

Cultural etiquette often defines how a business card should be given, received and treated – and this will differ from country to country. Before you visit a foreign country, ask a local how business cards are used. For example, here is the business card etiquette for Japan.

If you travel to Japan and meet people, business cards are expected and a 'must carry'. To show respect for your Japanese hosts, use double-sided business cards, one side printed in your native language, the other in Japanese. When business cards are exchanged, always present your business card (with Japanese language side face up) to the most senior member of the Japanese party first. Similarly, when receiving a business card, take it in both hands and say 'Thank you' or the Japanese for 'Thank you' – '*Hajimemashite*'. At the end of a meeting, remember to take all the business cards and put them in your business card holder. And, finally, never write notes on or play or fiddle with a Japanese business card.

Rules-based culture versus relationship-based culture

If you break the rules of rules-based cultures there are often heavy social and legal consequences – for example, jumping a queue in the UK, or crossing the road without using the pedestrian crossing in the USA – whereas relationship-based cultures place more value on the relationship than the rule. The relationship must be preserved first, rather than adhering to the society's rules. Having knowledge of whether a culture has a tendency to put the rule before the relationship is important for a networker. To generate opportunities within a relationship-based culture means it is even more about 'who you know or are related to' rather than 'what you know'.

Rules-based cultures	Relationship-based cultures
North America	Southern Europe (France, Italy, Spain, etc.)
UK	South America
Northern Europe	Middle East
Australia	

If you are networking within a relationship-based culture, make sure you spend more time on developing the relationship before starting to talk business.

Punctuality and time

Some cultures like people to be organised and to stay focused on the job at hand; others are quite comfortable with people multi-tasking and being spontaneous. Let me illustrate with two examples:

1 In the UK, if you entered someone's office and they were talking on the phone, you would sit down discreetly, avoid eye contact, and the person would close off their phone call before greeting you. By contrast, last year I did exactly the same in Rome and the speaker stood up, walked around the desk, greeted me with hugs and continued his telephone conversation!

2 Still in Rome, I later attended a meeting which began fully 40 minutes late! Then, during the meeting, people were freely making mobile phone calls, completing forms, which were totally unrelated to the meeting, *and* they addressed issues that were on the meeting agenda. It seemed to my British eyes that the meeting was a mess; however, everyone was quite at ease and the meeting achieved all it needed to do.

❝Check to see whether everyone else is relaxed❞

The moral is that, when you see something that makes you uncomfortable, check to see whether everyone else is relaxed and, if they are, simply go with the flow.

In some cultures, punctuality and order are very important. In these cultures, a host would be horrified if a guest turned up late or unannounced – would there be enough food for everyone? In fact, here in the UK, often you are given a window of time when you should turn up – how often do you see on an invite '18:30 for 19:00'? However, in cultures where punctuality and order are not as important, the host probably has made extra food, just in case a few extra people turn up. In Mediterranean Europe, times given can be approximately 15 minutes out, but in the Middle East and Africa a time given could mean any time that day.

Punctuality and order important	Punctuality and order less important
UK	South America
North America	Middle East
Asia	Africa
Australasia	Southern Europe

Relating to anyone you meet, regardless of where they are from

'Understand the differences; act on the commonalities.'

Andrew Masondo, African National Congress

A relationship is built upon shared values and trust. When you meet someone from a different economic, cultural or social background it is all too easy to see the differences. A business contact and very good friend of mine, David Stoch, is a very nice guy with this profile: he is young, male, single, from South Africa and lives alone in a suburb of London.[1] By contrast, I am older, female, British, married, have two kids and I live in the country. On the face of it, we are very different and from very different backgrounds. On a casual lunch one day, we discovered a mutual interest in classical and jazz music, and this has become the common ground that bonds us together when working on projects.

---

[1] www.meerkatpr.co.uk

When you meet someone different to you, use basic human shared values to connect with them. For example, pretty much everyone is proud of their family and home. A business owner almost always will be passionate about their business – and want to talk about it. BNI, the world's largest networking organisation, has operations in 44 countries. Each time they have launched in a new country they have been told that BNI wouldn't work there because the culture is different. The success of BNI tells a different story. They have found that business owners everywhere in the world are keen to work together to help each other grow their business – regardless of the dominant culture in which they are operating.

Most people will have hobbies and interests outside of work. What do they like to watch or listen to? What do they do to relax? What type of sport do they like to watch, follow or take part in?

If you look for differences, you will find them; if you look for the similarities you will also find them. This is why it is important when building a relationship with someone unfamiliar to you to look for the similarities and shared interests. Start by trusting the other person – trust their intentions and motivations, and open with a big happy smile – it will break all cultural barriers. You can always change your mind later.

Summary

When you are networking with people from different social, economic or cultural backgrounds, focus on areas of common interest and look for the similarities rather than the differences.

When networking in a place or country unfamiliar to your, research on the internet so that you know what to expect, and find a local guide or coach to help you fit in and understand appropriate behaviours and social etiquette.

To help engage and connect with people who do not speak your language, take the time to learn a few phrases of the local language.

Time is viewed differently by different cultures. In some cultures give yourself more time between meetings and appointments.

Watch and observe what the locals do when out meeting and greeting people. Follow their example and probably you won't go far wrong.

ACTION POINTS

■ Next time you visit a foreign country, buy a guide book and learn a few phrases of the native tongue.

■ For a week, try to spend an hour a day without using any jargon, slang or colloquialism when you talk.

■ If you visit a country regularly where the native tongue is not English, get the back of your business card translated into the country's native tongue.

■ Find an expat living in the UK and ask how different life and culture is in their home country.

■ Find someone at your work who is of a different social, economic or cultural background to you. Take the time to find out what you have in common, rather than looking for the differences. How easily does the relationship seem to form?

Further resources

Books

Morrison, T. and Conaway, W.A., *Kiss, Bow or Shake Hands*, Adams Media Corporation, 2006.

Trompenaars, F. and Hampden-Turner, C., *Riding the Waves of Culture: Understanding cultural diversity in business*, Nicholas Brealey Publishing, third edition, 2012.

Websites and blogs

Cyborlink www.cyborlink.com

Executive Planet www.executiveplanet.com

Kwintessential www.kwintessential.co.uk/resources/country-profiles.html

4

Putting your joined-up approach to networking into action

So far in this book we have looked at the behaviours, attitudes and skills needed to be a successful networker. In the last part of the book we are going to put it all together and build a personal networking strategy and action plan for you, to help you achieve career and business success.

14

Building your own successful joined-up networking strategy

What topics are covered in this chapter?

- How to build a successful joined-up networking strategy
- How to build a network of people who help you achieve your business and career goals
- Where to meet great people for your network
- How to measure your effectiveness as a networker

'98 per cent of people have generated business via word of mouth, only 3 per cent have a strategy to do so.'

BNI research

What do we mean by a networking strategy?

Effective business networking is the process of finding, building and maintaining mutually beneficial relationships. Your networking strategy details how you will achieve your goals via your networking activities.

A clear and concise networking strategy will allow you to make the decisions as to *what* networking activities you will do; it is your *plan* for connecting to important people. If you implement your plan, you will achieve your networking goals. There are five steps involved in creating your networking strategy (see Figure 14.1):

Step 1 Goals – decide what you want to achieve from your networking activities.

Step 2 Audit – assess the suitability of your current networking activities to help you achieve your networking goals.

Step 3 Find – identify people to add in to your network.

Step 4 Build – progress and deepen the right relationships.

Step 5 Maintain – keep your relationships strong and working for you.

If you complete each stage, your networking plan will almost write itself.

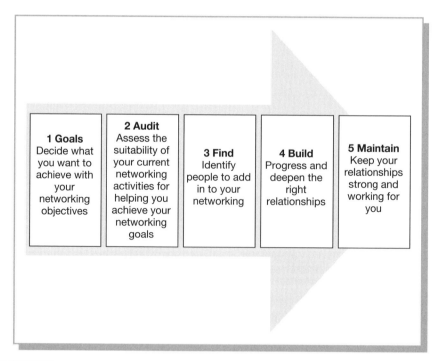

figure 14.1   The five steps to building your own personal networking strategy

Step 1 Goals

'The number one reason why some people get work done faster is because they are absolutely clear about their goals and objectives and don't deviate from them.'

Brian Tracy, author of Eat That Frog![1]

❝Your personal networking journey may take you outside of your comfort zone❞

Take a moment to reflect on why you picked up this book and decided to read it. What was it particularly about business networking, your business or your career, that compelled you to read a book on the subject? There has to be some personal motivation on your part to understand more about networking – most people don't get up in the morning and decide, 'I know, I will read a book on business networking'. Your personal networking journey may take you outside of your comfort zone and possibly force you to confront some of your personal fears. At these points in time, knowing why you are doing what you are doing, and the prize waiting at the end of it, often will mean the difference between success and failure.

So, let's explore your motivation to improve your knowledge and skills about business networking.

- What are you hoping to achieve more of, for less time and effort, by improving your ability to network?
- If I could wave a magic wand and grant you one wish, what would you ask for? More business, a promotion, a better job, a bigger support network?

'Only about 3 per cent of adults have clear written goals. These people accomplish five and ten times as much as people of equal or better education and ability but have, for whatever reason, taken the time to write out exactly what it is they want.'

Brian Tracy, author of Eat That Frog!

It is likely that your motivation is linked to your business, career or personal goals. If you don't have a clear goal in your mind, it's going to make it very difficult to make your networking activities actually happen, because you won't have sufficient motivation to do any or some of these things:

---

[1] Tracy, B., *Eat that Frog! Get more of the important things done – today!*, Berrett-Koehler Publishers, Inc, revised edn, 2013.

- Make the effort to go into LinkedIn regularly and join in the conversation.
- Go into Twitter daily.
- Head out to a networking event after a long, hard day in the office.
- Pick up the phone and speak to someone you haven't connected to for a while.

Close your eyes for a few moments and try to visualise what success you want to achieve. What does your inner voice say to you? What do you see in your mind's eye? What feelings are you experiencing?

Then, complete this sentence:

My networking strategy will help me achieve _____ (fill in with what it will help you achieve) *by* _____ (fill in with a date by when you want to achieve this).

Here are some examples of how your networking goals can be linked to business, career or personal goals:

My networking strategy will help me find a new job of equal or better pay, less than an hour's travel from my house, working for a retailing company, by Dec 31st.

To build a client portfolio worth £500k within 2 years, I will use my network to generate 4 new referrals every quarter.

To establish a new office in Bristol next year, I will build a personal network in that city during this current year. This network will be of potential clients that the new office will need, and also will assist in identifying new (local) recruits.

My career goal is to move out of sales and into an events management role within 6–18 months' time. This will require me to network with people in that industry and become known.

My networking activities in the local community, particularly with the other parents at the school gate, will help me out when I have diary clashes and need someone else to pick up my kids from school.

Now, take a look at what you have just written and be honest with yourself.

1 Is this your goal? You are far more likely to achieve your personal goal if you make your goal your own, rather than trying to achieve someone else's goals for you.

2 Is this goal realistic? For example, growing your business by ten times in the space of three months by networking alone is probably not realistic.

3 Does your goal have a fixed date? Summer is not a fixed date; 31st July is a fixed date.

4 Can you measure your goal to know whether you have succeeded or failed? 'Be a better networker' is not a measurable specific goal. 'Win five new clients for the next three months' is measurable *and* specific.

5 Is your goal *specific*? Can your goal be visualised? For example, you can visualise easily a monthly report showing five new clients being won each month.

If you have answered 'No' to any of these five questions, then go back and revisit your networking goal(s) until you have it right.

---

case study   Rosemary

Rosemary was a freelance trainer who was keen to build up her reputation and profile in her niche of marketing agencies. She gave herself a networking goal to use Twitter to build up relationships with journalists to get coverage in the marketing trade press. As a result of this strategy, she has formed strong relationships with five journalists who write regularly in the marketing trade press. Typically, Rosemary will find that she is quoted in an article by one of these journalists every couple of months.

Step 2 Audit

Many people think that they have to build a network from scratch. Actually, each of us naturally has our own network – and, for many of us, there will be some great contacts within our current network who will be able to help us achieve our networking goals. For example, Robert was a long-term member of his golf club. It was only after sitting down with a member of the club, David, that he realised David was a senior decision maker in a company that he wanted as a client.

Just because you have a network and are networking all the time, doesn't mean to say that you are doing it in an effective manner, i.e. spending time with the right people in the right places. This is why the second stage of building a networking strategy is to do a networking audit. After all, you don't want to change anything that is working.

The best way to do a networking audit is to draw out your network map. Begin literally by mapping out your ideal network (see Figure 14.2). It's an exercise that will really help to focus you on *who* you want to meet, and how these people are going to help you achieve your business and career goals.

This may sound rather calculating or manipulative. However, it is a tool to help you focus on how you will spend your networking time. Let's be frank here: how many times have you turned up to a networking event without knowing why you were there and whom you would benefit from meeting? Was it a productive use of your time? A network map will help you visualise your networking time. It also has the additional benefit of helping you

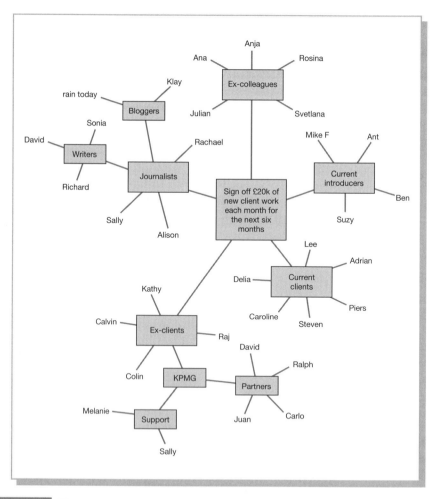

figure 14.2   **Example of a networking map**

prioritise your networking activities, because now you truly understand why you are networking and why it is important to your future career or business health.

Most people, after completing their networking map, realise that their *current* network contains many of the types of people that can help them actively achieve their networking goals.

Analysing the state of your network

There are three main activities in the growth of a productive network:

■ building connections

■ deepening existing relationships

■ pruning connections.

A successful networker will be doing all three activities simultaneously. However, there will be times when there will need to be more focus on one of the three activities. For example, when I had my first child, I switched my networking focus so that I could build up a network of local first-time mums to support me through my transition to motherhood. After five years as a business owner, 80 per cent of my networking time and effort is now spent deepening existing relationships, rather than actively cultivating new connections.

As a busy professional or business owner you need to focus your networking efforts on the connections that give you the greatest rate of return – whether that is support, friendship, answers or new business. It is impossible to keep every relationship strong and current; inevitably some people in your network naturally will fall away. Very occasionally, you may need to reassess a relationship and prune it from your network: perhaps the relationship has gone sour, circumstances have changed or your credibility is being damaged by being close to this person. At its most severe, pruning may involve disconnecting yourself from a contact on a social network. Pruning your network may sound a drastic step, but it is very similar to the reasons why we prune a fruit tree – the act of pruning makes the fruit tree stronger and better prepared to yield a bigger crop next year.

Look at your network map. Is your network in a state to help you achieve your networking goals easily? What approximate percentage of time do you need to spend on building, deepening or pruning? What activities are you doing – such as membership of a professional networking group – that are helping you connect with the right types of people, i.e. hubs?

■ What activities are you doing that are helping you achieve your career and business goals?

■ What activities are not working for you?

■ What activities should you start doing right now?

Step 3 Find

Identifying who you need in your network

In Chapter 7 we coined the phrase 'A-lister' to define the person who is most likely to be able to help you achieve your goals. However, we will begin by profiling your ideal client, since this is the key to choosing the most appropriate A-lister.

> **Tip**
>
> If you are reading this chapter and thinking 'but I want my network to help me accelerate my career, not generate business', you are still involved in selling something. It just so happens that the product or service you are selling is you, and your ideal client is a new boss or new employer.

Thinking about your ideal client, customer or employer, how much do you know about their:

■ industry sector

■ position or job title

■ reading preferences

■ social networking site memberships

■ hobbies or interests outside of work

■ habits, behaviours, personality types?

Connectors

In his book *The Tipping Point*, Malcolm Gladwell identified a special type of networker called a 'connector'.[2] These are people who are able to maintain a high level of influence naturally within a network of people – significantly bigger than that of the average person. Their large networks span many different professions, social and cultural circles. But, more importantly for

---

[2] Gladwell, M., *The Tipping Point*, Abacus, 40th Anniversary edn, 2013.

networkers, connectors make a habit of regularly introducing people within their networks. Gladwell discovered that true connectors are quite rare – they number about one person in several thousand.

Whilst a connector may not, on first sight, naturally be an A-lister for you, the sheer size and influence they wield within their network means they have the potential to regularly introduce you to the people you do want to meet.

Gatekeepers

Your A-listers are very likely to be people who are 'gatekeepers' to a network that contains a high percentage of your ideal client. Gatekeepers already have a large and well-established network, and are seen to be at the 'hub' of this network. To make your networking as efficient as possible, your aim needs to be to find and generate strong relationships with as many gatekeepers to your ideal client as possible. For example, Sharon Gaskin, managing director of The Trainers Training Company, is a gatekeeper to a network of more than 1,000 self-employed trainers.[3]

"Your aim needs to be to find and generate strong relationships"

If you identify an A-lister who is a gatekeeper, you need to develop a strong relationship with them, so that you increase the probability of receiving referrals. This is why it pays to focus your networking time and attention on A-listers who happen to be gatekeepers.

To help you think about where to look for gatekeepers, fill in a client analysis worksheet (see overleaf) for each of your ideal clients, and who may be well connected to them, based on their personal preferences. (This worksheet is available to download at www.joinedupnetworking.com.)

Take a look at your client analysis worksheet to help you identify who should be in your network:

■ Who is well connected to my target client?

■ Who do I know who is a gatekeeper to a large network of my target client?

■ Do I know any connectors?

When you are networking, you need to be on the lookout for ideal clients, new A-listers, connectors and gatekeepers.

---

[3] www.thetrainerstrainingcompany.co.uk

	Ideal client	*Where will they 'hang out'?*	*Who else will be connected to them?*
Industry sector	Accountant	ICAEW events	Lawyers
		Chambers of Commerce events	IFAs
		4N and BNI	
		Professional seminars	
Age	30–60		
Reading preferences		*Accountancy Age*	
Social networking site memberships	Accounting Web		
	Twitter		
	UK Business Forums		
Hobbies or interests outside of work		Potential school governor?	
		Scouts	
		Sporting club member	
Habits, behaviours, personality types	Introverted, likes numbers		
Family status		School events	Parents at the school

Step 4 Build

The Excedia 5-level relationship model

The aim with your networking activity is to deepen those relationships that matter to you. Most people realise that not everyone is created equal in their network. In fact, the state of your relationship can be described in a five-level relationship model (see Figure 14.3), which allows you to categorise the state of your relationship:

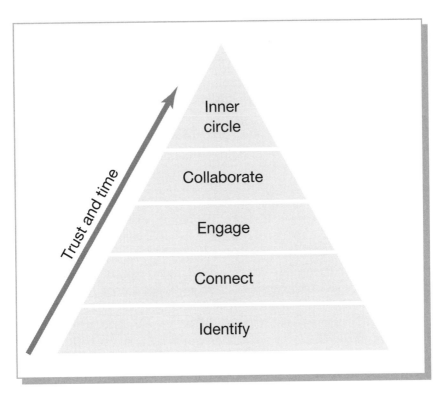

figure 14.3   The Excedia 5-level relationship model

Level 1 Identify at this level, you have just become aware of this contact. Maybe someone has mentioned them in conversation or perhaps you have seen a tweet of theirs. Or perhaps they are on an attendance list of an event you are attending.

Level 2 Connect at this point you have met, physically or virtually, a contact, and started a one- or two-way conversation; i.e. you have connected. For example, you may have talked to them at a face-to-face networking event, or exchanged some tweets or posts within an online forum.

Level 3 Engage at this point, you have taken a conscious decision to strengthen the relationship, and move beyond small talk. This means that you have taken the time to have a one-to-one meeting with them, whether in person, or by phone.

Level 4 Collaborate the trust has built within the relationship to the point where you have agreed to help each other, pass referrals and, potentially, actively look for ways to work together.

Level 5 Inner circle the relationship is now such that you have worked together, and regularly recommend each other's services. There is a strong possibility that your relationship has moved from a purely professional relationship into a personal friendship.

---

case study   Tony

Tony was an ambitious surveyor in a large engineering consultancy. He was keen to grow his client portfolio to advance his career within this firm. He noticed the firm was becoming increasingly successful in renewable energy projects. As a result, he actively built his network and key contacts around people, both inside and outside of his firm, with an interest or a specialism in renewable energy. Over a few years his investment in these relationships really started to pay off, as through these relationships he was bringing in new business opportunities regularly for the firm as a whole.

---

case study   David Kaye

David is known throughout the retail world as the Go-To Expert for legal expertise. His relationship with key contacts in the retail world, which included Sir Philip Green's CEO Ian Grabiner, was responsible for the growth of his practice and client base. Along the way his small, niche firm Clairmonts, with a team of 15, worked with many retailing household names such as Arcadia, Birthdays (Clinton Cards), Reality, a division of GUS (Great Universal Stores), Sports Division (who acquired Olympus), Gadget Shop, USC, d2, MJM International Ltd/Ultimo Lingerie and many others.

Relationship plans

You want to have in place a relationship plan for all your A-listers and, potentially, some of your B-listers (see Figure 14.4). A relationship plan:

■ details what you know about the person and what more you want to know about them

■ contains the desired level of contact you want

■ indicates what you would like to achieve because of your relationship.

NAME	John Brown	LINKEDIN & TWITTER	www.linkedin.com/in/johnbrown @jcbrown
PHONE	01234 567 8910	WEBSITE	www.johnbrownLLP.co.uk
EMAIL	jcbrown@johnbrownLLP.co.uk	ADDRESS	Business house, 100, Any street, New Town, AB10 9CD
ROLE	Owner	COMPANY	John Brown LLP
FREQUENCY OF CONTACT?		In person: every 6 months, phone calls quarterly, email monthly, twitter account monitored daily	
CURRENT & DESIRED RELATIONSHIP LEVEL (out of 5)		Current = 3, desired = 4	
THEIR GOALS & OBJECTIVES		Double the size of their revenue & maintain profit margin in next 2 years Identify 2 assistant solicitors to delegate down too	
THEIR INTERESTS OUTSIDE OF WORK		Golf, fine dining, Spurs supporter	
FAMILY SITUATION		Married with 2 teenage children, Stephen (13), Alex (15)	
HOW CAN I HELP THEM?		Reduce tax bill, and start to provide management accounts quarterly	
WHAT CONTENT DO THEY WELCOME ME SENDING THEM?		Our monthly newsletter & articles which they may find interesting	
RELATIONSHIP NEXT STEPS		Organise next lunch & suggest a round of golf	

figure 14.4   A blank relationship plan

It's all very well having relationship plans for the folks who matter to you. However, you need to implement these plans. Every month, review all of your relationship plans and check that you have three months of the right level of contact planned into your diary. Then, extend your relationship plans by another month.

Tip

If you have admin assistance available, use it to book in your planned meetings and the events you will attend.

Mike Briercliffe

Mike is a natural connector, and is the hub of many different personal and professional networks. He uses various online networking tools to manage his contacts at the different stages of his relationship with them.

Level 1 Identify over the past five years Twitter has become Mike's main mechanism for identifying new potential members for his network.

Level 2 Engage when Mike starts to have a conversation with a potential connection, he will strengthen the relationship by inviting them to connect with him on LinkedIn.

Level 3 Strengthen at the point that the trust starts to build and Mike sees some potential in the relationship going further, he will take the relationship offline and suggest a phone call or one-to-one meeting.

Level 4 Collaborate Mike will use both LinkedIn and Twitter to maintain a regular conversation with those people he trusts and will recommend.

Level 5 Inner circle at this point, Mike has worked with this person, trusts them explicitly and they will have been invited to join his personal social network on Ning and black book of trusted contacts.

Helen Stothard

Helen runs HLS Business Solutions, a virtual assistant business. Helen's team and clients are spread right across the UK and Europe. She has never advertised her business and has generated all her clients, suppliers and team members via her networking activities. Helen's sole aim when networking is to build strong relationships with advocates for her and her business.

Level 1 Identify Helen initially meets potential members for her network from online forums, Twitter and a community of virtual assistants called VASG.

Level 2 Engage Helen will start conversations on the online forums and Twitter. She builds up the relationships first by proactively sharing advice and knowledge.

Level 3 Strengthen normally, Helen's network will initiate a conversation with her – generally via Skype, but, as many in her network are more than an hour's travel away, very rarely in person.

Level 4 Collaborate when Helen has started to work for, recommend or use a person in her network, she aims to find a way to meet in person – often when her clients are holidaying near to her or she will deliberately plan a weekend away near to someone she wants to meet in person.

Level 5 Inner circle for Helen's trusted contacts, she connects with them socially and uses Facebook to keep the relationship personal as well as professional.

Deciding where to network

'A successful networker will fish in a pond well stocked with big fishes.'

Jon Baker, co-author of The Go-To Expert

❝There is no right or wrong answer about where to network❞

Once you have identified who you want to meet and why you want to meet them, you need to identify where you are going to meet them.

If you need some ideas on where you can meet people, look back to Chapters 4 and 5 for all the different online and face-to-face networking available. There is no right or wrong answer about where to network – however, for your networking to be effective, first you need to be clear on what you want to achieve from your networking.

Tip

To find an online forum for a certain type of person or interest, do a Google search for 'online forum xxx', e.g. online forum lawyers, online forum parents.

There is no easy way to find the best places to network. You need to be pre-pared to do your research and experiment with events and groups, as not every group, event or forum will work for everyone – see Table 14.1.

■ Ask around and do some internet searches, i.e. where do your competitors and peers hang out?

■ Attend a few networking groups as a guest.

■ Attend some events hosted by your professional association.

> **Tip**
>
> To find local networking events and groups targeted at small businesses, do a Google search for 'business networking xxxx' or 'professional networking xxxx', e.g. business networking Bedford.

Table 14.1 Types of networking best suited to different networking goals

You want to:	Try:
Enhance your profile	Mix-and-mingle type events, Twitter, online forums, speaking at events, professional association events, writing a blog
Generate new business	Referral generation clubs (particularly if you target small businesses), Twitter, blogging, conferences
Find answers and solutions	Mastermind groups, online forums, professional association events, reading blogs
Build your community	Voluntary, special interest or community groups, mastermind groups, online forums, social events
Find a new job	Social events, professional association events, LinkedIn, blogging

There is a plethora of online networking sites around (see Chapter 5). The vast range of online networking sites gives the networker the option of using different sites to categorise the state of their relationship with a person. For example, I will connect with most people on LinkedIn, and follow most genuine people back on Twitter, but I will connect with people on my personal Facebook account only if I would be happy to invite them to my house for dinner.

Bryony Thomas

Bryony has developed a joined-up networking strategy that has allowed her to source locally based clients successfully for her marketing consultancy, Watertight Marketing. The aim of her networking strategy is to develop a strong, locally based network of clients, referrers and suppliers. She has achieved great results by applying her joined-up networking strategy ruthlessly and consistently over the past two years. This rigour and discipline have allowed her to build a business that has billed over £400,000 through its network of marketing suppliers in its first two years of business.

She uses Twitter to complement her locally based face-to-face networking. When she is out and about (both virtually and physically) she looks actively for like-minded local professionals to engage in conversation. Her Twitter conversation is a mixture of professional, for example her thoughts on marketing, and personal, such as her reactions to the weekend's big television show. LinkedIn is Bryony's equivalent of her little black book. Every single person on her LinkedIn profile she has either worked with or met in a professional capacity.

Step 5 Maintain

Think back to your friends at school. How many of them are you still in contact with? Now, those that you have lost contact with, do you feel able to pick up the phone and speak with them? I'm guessing not. So, what has made the difference with your friends from school who you feel able to still pick up the phone and talk to?

Yes, regular communication. Without regular communication, your relationships will slip back and lose their usefulness. Therefore, a key part of your networking strategy needs to be how you will keep in touch with your network.

One of the best ways of keeping in touch with the important people in your network is through sending them and sharing with them valuable content. This could be articles or recordings made by you or others.

Measuring your effectiveness

'Nobody gets paid for networking. We all get paid on the results of our networking.'

Rob Brown, motivational speaker and networking expert

Successful networking takes time, money and effort. This means that you need to measure where you are having the most success with your networking efforts so you can replicate the things you are doing right and increase the effectiveness of your future results.

❛❛You need to measure where you are having the most success❜❜

Look back to your networking goals that you set at the beginning of this chapter. How will you know when you are being successful? For example, if your prime aim is to secure a new job, you will know if you are being successful when you are talking with relevant companies and hiring managers who have a vacancy to fill.

What can you measure, and how regularly should you assess the effectiveness of your networking? For example you could measure:

■ the number of A-listers in your network where your relationship level is 3 or above

■ the number of people within your target market with whom you have a one-to-one conversation

■ the amount of business you receive via your network, and who the business comes from

■ the amount of help you receive from people within your network.

Let's look at a real-life example:

The networking goal: In April I set myself a goal to find a publisher by 31 October via my network, for the book I wanted to write on networking.

The networking strategy: I had two main parts to my networking strategy:

1 Meet business book authors to gain introductions to their publishers.

2 Become known as an expert on networking so that a publisher would find me and ask me to write a book on networking for them.

The measurements of effectiveness I used:

▦ Number of business book authors I meet, and progress the relationship to a level 3.

▦ Introductions to publishers.

▦ Number of email and phone conversations with publishers.

▦ Number of articles written on the subject of networking, which showcased me as an author of networking.

▦ Number of reads of articles I had written on the subject of networking.

The result: Six weeks after setting my networking goal, I had gained four introductions to publishers, but was approached to write this book by Liz Gooster of Financial Times Prentice Hall. She had 'found' me by reading several of my articles on networking, which I had posted on Business Zone. Since this initial meeting, Liz and I have built and maintained a very strong relationship. As a result of this relationship, Liz then went on to publish my second book *How to Make Partner and Still Have a Life*, and has also published many of my network's books.

Summary

There are five stages to building your networking strategy:

1 Set goals.

2 Audit your current networking activity and contacts.

3 Find people to add into your network.

4 Build the relationships with people in your network.

5 Maintain the relationships in your network.

To be effective, your network needs to contain people with whom you have a genuine connection, that is where your relationship is at a minimum of level 3, i.e. *strengthen, collaborate* or *inner circle*. For someone to be a genuine connection there needs to be trust present and they would happily recommend your services to others.

Finding the right place to network will take time and an element of experimentation. Constantly make adjustments to your strategy and plan as you grow and learn.

ACTION POINTS

■ Write a networking goal that will help you achieve personal, business and career success. Now demonstrate your commitment and hold yourself accountable by telling at least three people about your goal.

■ Who in your current network can help you achieve your networking goal – or introduce you to someone who can help you achieve your goal?

■ Write down everything you know about your ideal client and people well connected to them. What could you do to find out more about them?

■ Draw out your network map. What insights have you gained from the map? What could you do to help increase the effectiveness of your network and networking activities?

■ Who do you know who may be a gatekeeper to your target market? How can you make contact with them and build a strong relationship?

■ Who do you know who is always introducing people and seems to know everyone? They may be a natural connector. How can you strengthen your relationship with them?

■ Tell three members of your family or friends about your business interests and ask them who they know who can help you.

■ Think about the A-listers within your network. For each A-lister, analyse the state of the relationship. What level of relationship do you have with each of them? What do you need to do to strengthen the relationship?

■ Find three new places to network where you will meet your target market.

■ Thinking about your networking goal, what can you measure to determine how successful you are becoming?

Further resources

Books

Gladwell, M., *The Tipping Point*, Abacus, 40th Anniversary edition, 2013.

Misner, I. and Donovan, M.R., *The 29% Solution*, Olive Tree Press, 2008.

Tracy, B. *Eat That Frog! Get more of the important things done – today!*, Berrett-Koehler Publishers, fully revised and updated edition, 2013.

Websites

Rob Brown's blog www.therobbrown.com/connected-professional/

Joined Up Networking www.joinedupnetworking.com for worksheets to help:

■ set your personal networking goals

■ identify your target client and A-lister

■ measure your networking success.

15

Writing your joined-up networking plan

What topics are covered in this chapter?

- How to use your networking opportunity score to focus your networking efforts
- What to do first to get started with online networking
- How to find the best local networking events
- How to choose the right social networking site for your networking strategy
- How to write a networking action plan

In the previous chapter we looked at the steps needed to build a successful joined-up networking strategy. In this chapter we will focus on building a realistic plan to achieve your goals.

Using your networking opportunity score to focus your efforts

In Chapter 2 we identified four elements needed for a successful networking strategy: credibility, personal brand, visibility and social capital. Whilst it may be impossible to predict where your next opportunity, e.g. job offer, new assignment, new client, speaking engagement, will come from, focusing on these four elements will help you to improve the likelihood of you generating opportunities via your network.

You will recall, in Chapter 2, we linked these four elements by the following equation:

Opportunity = Credibility × (Personal brand + Visibility + Social capital)

where

Opportunity represents an opportunity score. The greater this number, the higher the likelihood of opportunities coming to you.

Credibility = your personal credibility.

Personal brand = the marketability and strength of your personal brand.

Visibility = visibility to your target market.

Social Capital = the amount of social capital you have generated within your network.

If you haven't already done so, thinking about your current networking goals, calculate your opportunity score using Table 15.1. Remember that there is no ideal score. Of course, the higher your score, the more likely it is that you will generate opportunities via your network. What Table 15.1 gives you is a way of focusing on activities that are the most likely to help you generate more opportunities from your networking activities.

Which of the four ingredients for a successful networking strategy do you need to spend time on to increase your likelihood of generating opportunities via your network? For example, if you are low on visibility, what do you need to do to increase your profile and top-of-the-mind visibility to your target audience?

You may like to brainstorm actions to improve your scores in each of the four areas (see Table 15.2). (This sheet is available as a downloadable worksheet at www.joinedupnetworking.com.)

What are three actions you could do to improve your opportunity score to help you achieve your networking goals? Write down these actions and set yourself a deadline to achieve them.

Table 15.1 Calculate your opportunity score

Score	Credibility	Personal brand	Visibility	Social capital
	The extent to which you deliver on your promises and 'walk your walk' and 'talk your talk'	The marketability and strength of your personal brand	Your profile amongst your target market	The influence and reach you have within your network
1	You have no track record in your specialist area, and are unlikely to write or talk about your specialist subject.	You are not distinguishable amongst your peers.	Your target market has never heard of you.	Influential only amongst relatives and immediate work colleagues.
2	You may write or talk about your specialist subject. Some people ask your opinion, but often they are asking others ahead of you.	You are known amongst your close network as 'the person' who you need to talk to for 'y'.	Your target market becomes aware of you.	Strong influence of up to 50 people.
3	You write and talk regularly about your specialist subject and are building up a small client list.	You have an active social media presence, and are known amongst your wide network as 'the person' who you need to talk to for 'y'.	Your name is known within your target market and you may have a small following on social media (<1,000 followers).	Strong influence of 51–150 people.
4	You write and talk about your specialist subject regularly and have a well-stocked client list, with a few people using you as a trusted advisor.	You may have a book published, and have a very active social media presence – via blogging and social networking sites. Journalists occasionally will quote you. Your personal brand is now becoming stronger than your business brand.	Your name is well known within your target market, and you are likely to have a medium-sized following (2,000 followers or connections) on social media.	Strong influence of 151–500 people.
5	You are in constant demand to write and talk about your specialist subject. You have an impressive client list, and there are many people who use you as a trusted advisor.	You have written books, published articles, appeared on TV, presented at major conferences and are a household name within your industry or area of specialism.	Your name is widely known within your target market, and you are likely to have a large following (10,000 followers or connections) on social media.	Strong influence of 501+ people.

How to get started with online networking

❝Here is my eight-step quick guide to getting started❞

Over the past four years I've met many people who want to network online but don't know how to get started. If you are one of these people, here is my eight-step quick guide to getting started with online networking.

1 Write a short profile about yourself, making sure you include relevant keywords within the description. (See Chapter 8 for how to write an online profile.)

This is my short profile, which I use as the basis for all the online profiles and biographies about me:

Heather Townsend helps professionals become the Go-To Expert. Unusually for someone with an Engineering Degree, Heather accidentally became a writer and used her knowledge on social media to write the current best-selling and award-winning book on networking, The FT Guide to Business Networking. *Since then, Heather has co-authored two more books,* How to Make Partner and Still Have a Life *and* The Go-To Expert. *People talk about her frequently as someone who really knows her stuff – which may be the reason she has, over the last decade, worked with over 300 partners, and coached and trained over 2,000 professionals at every level of the UK's most ambitious professional practices.*

2 Then find a good-quality but low-resolution professional head-and-shoulders photo. It is worth having at least two professional photos available for you to use, for example, if you operate more than one Twitter account.

3 Join LinkedIn, Twitter, Facebook, Google+ and a maximum of two other online forums.

4 Fill out your profile for the online networking sites that you have joined and follow the site's suggestions to connect with people you may already know on the site. For example, LinkedIn will go through your Microsoft Outlook and online address book to find people you already know on LinkedIn, and send a request to connect.

5 Start your own blog and write about a subject that showcases your credibility. Update your blog at least once a month. Use Twitterfeed to connect your blog to your social networking status updates, e.g. Twitter, LinkedIn and Facebook.

Table 15.2 Brainstorming actions to improve your opportunity score

To increase my opportunity score, I could...

Credibility	Personal brand	Visibility	Social capital
■ Start a blog on my specialist subject	■ Start a blog on my specialist subject	■ Aim to meet at least one new person a week	■ Commit to following up with everyone I meet within 48 hours
■ Talk to my current clients to find out why they chose to work with me	■ Write my short online profile/bio	■ Spend an hour profiling and researching my ideal client	■ Join the committee of my professional association's local branch
■ Set up an RSS feed reader with blogs that are within my specialist area, and comment on one blog a week	■ Get a new professional photo taken of me	■ Ask my peers which events and groups they find helpful	■ Review the list of my A-listers and identify who I need to spend time with strengthening the relationship
■ Identify someone within my current company who I could work with on an assignment to increase my credibility	■ Speak to my colleagues and ask them what they believe that I stand for	■ Tag all my contacts in my address book and LinkedIn as A-, B- or C-lister	
■ Find an online networking site where I can showcase my credentials		■ Commit to speaking to an A-lister at least once a week	
		■ Join a new networking group	

6 Introduce yourself to other people within your online networking sites.

7 Do a Google search for bloggers who write about subjects that are interesting to you, or subjects that match your specialism. Add the RSS feed from the blog into your RSS feed reader, for example Feedly.

8 Set aside a minimum of 30 minutes each day to go into your online networking sites and read the blogs in your RSS feed reader. Aim to complete the following each day:

■ A status update relevant to the audience on the site, for example keep your status updates on LinkedIn very professional, but light, personal and social on Facebook.

■ A way of helping out someone on the site, for example answering a question or connecting two people together.

■ Find up to five people every day to start a conversation with, whether this is commenting on a blog or chatting to someone on Twitter, answering a 'LinkedIn question' or joining in a discussion on an online forum.

■ Share interesting content with your connections on your social networking sites.

How to find the best online networking sites

In Chapter 5 we identified all the different types of online networking sites available to the networker. With this amount of choice, it can be difficult to know where to spend your time online.

Before you can assess a site, you need to know what you want to achieve by maintaining a presence on that site. Or whether you want to maintain a visible presence at all – as there will be times when you have a very specific need. For example, there are many user forums available with a very specific goal, such as user forums for your satellite navigation system, or developer forums for a range of Wordpress themes. Personally I have used these sites when I have a specific query rather than phoning customer services – and these sites often remove the need for a front-line customer service function for a company.

Here are a few ideas to find the right online networking site for you:

■ Do a Google search on 'online forum xxx', where xxx could be an industry, type of person you want to meet or product you need help with.

- Have a look at how many members are active on the site – you are looking for a minimum of 1,000 members.

- Read the quality of the posts – is this a site that will enhance your credibility and personal brand by maintaining a regular presence?

- See how many of your competitors are contributing regularly to discussion threads. Too many of your peers may mean that the site is saturated with your particular specialism and it may take a while to build up a meaningful level of visibility and credibility.

- Ask questions on places like Twitter or LinkedIn to find online networking sites that other people rate.

How to find the best local networking events

Similar to finding the best online networking site to spend time on, there is no quick and easy answer to finding the best local networking events. One group or event may be perfect for one business or individual but ineffective for another. This is because people always will have personalised networking goals and networking preferences.

❝Never take someone else's word that a networking event or group is great❞

The best way to find potentially great local networking events is to ask around your network. Ideally, you want to find a group or event where you are made to feel welcome and given plenty of opportunities to get to know people. As you need to remember, effective networking is not about passing business, it's about building up relationships with people.

So, you need to know what you are looking for – in terms of both your own networking objectives and also what makes a good, vibrant group. Never take someone else's word that a networking event or group is great – always visit a couple of times as a guest before committing to joining or attending regularly.

'Your decision to join a networking group should never be solely based on how nice the group is.'

Robert Watson, Valuable Comment

When you visit a group or event, take a temperature check on the atmosphere in the room:

- Are there plenty of regulars?

■ Is the group knowledgeable and well connected?

■ Are there plenty of people who have been attending the group or event for a long time?

■ Is there energy and enthusiasm from the group or event's leader?

■ Are you made to feel welcome?

■ Do the regulars come up to talk to you?

■ Do people look as if they are having fun?

If you are attending a referral generation group, then also look out for the following signs:

■ What proportion of people are bringing referrals to the group?

■ Is the membership growing or declining?

How to join up your networking activities effectively

In my research for this book, I discovered that the most successful networkers don't see any distinction between online or face-to-face networking – it's all about choosing the right medium to connect with the right person.

There are two big hurdles for networkers when thinking about joining up their networking activities: fear of the unknown and knowing how to get started. There is a newer breed of networkers emerging who have grown up with Facebook and know how to engage naturally online, but struggle to work a room. Likewise, there is the often older, skilled face-to-face networker who is very comfortable with working a room and building rapport with others, but doesn't know where or how to start with online networking. As I have found out personally, there are greater rewards available to the networker who is prepared to embrace a joined-up networking strategy.

To identify how you can join up your networking activities effectively, use the tools and processes worksheet (downloadable at www.joinedupnet working.com) to brainstorm ideas of how you can progress your contacts through the relationship levels. See Table 15.3 (overleaf) for an example.

Table 15.3 Progressing your contacts through the relationship levels

Relationship level	Online tools and processes	Face-to-face tools and processes
1: Identify	Twitter Accounting Web LinkedIn Answers	Chamber of Commerce events Inter-company socials
2: Connect	Follow and chat on Twitter Request to connect on LinkedIn Use questions in my blog posts Answer questions in my blog post	Email exchange Send postcard to potential A-listers I meet Join a mastermind group
3: Engage	Exchange private messages on Twitter and LinkedIn Connect on Skype Invite to connect on another social networking site	Phone call Skype video call In-person meeting
4: Collaborate	Share blog links LinkedIn closed group	Phone call Skype video call In-person meeting Join a small project team
5: Inner circle	Twitter – 'inner circle' list membership Connect on personal Facebook page	Monthly meetings and diarised conversations

Writing your networking action plan

It's time now to write your networking action plan. You may like to use our networking action plan worksheet to help you, which is downloadable at www.joinedupnetworking.com (see also below).

Any networking action plan needs to contain the following items:

- Your networking goals and objectives.
- Your strategy – how you will achieve your networking goal.
- Your success criteria – how do you know when you are being successful with your networking?
- Your A-listers and how you will meet them and stay in touch with them.
- An assessment of the networking 'assets' you have at the moment.

My networking goal:	
■ Find a new job as a learning and development specialist, within an hour's travel from home	
My networking strategy: (who I need to meet to achieve my networking goal)	
1 Meet learning & development (L&D) directors, and HR directors of companies locally 2 Increase my network of UK-based HR professionals 3 Blog and tweet about leadership within professional services 4 Meet recruitment consultants specialising in placing learning and development professionals	
Who do I know already? (who could help me)	
Work colleagues (current or ex)	*Friends, family, neighbours*
1 My ex-boss Jo 2 My team	1 Next door neighbour works for NHS?
Old friends from school or college	*Suppliers, customers, clients*
1 Sarah 2 James	1 External trainers – Bridget
People I have met on training courses and at conferences	*People I know from non-work-related organisations I belong to*
	1 CIPD local branch committee
People in my address book	*Twitter followers, LinkedIn connections, Facebook friends or connections on other social networking sites*
Success criteria: (how do I know when I am being successful?)	
1 I have increased the number of HR professionals I am connected to on LinkedIn from 15 to 300+ 2 I will be getting told about one new potential job every week 3 I will get an introduction to an HR or L&D director every month 4 I will have a new job, within an hour's travel of home, within 6 months	

Current and future opportunities for networking		
Organisations I belong to		*Where do friends and colleagues network?*
1 CIPD local branch committee		**1** Need to find out
Future conferences, training courses, project groups		*Online networking sites*

Who are my A-listers?	Where or how to meet them?	How to stay in touch?
Recruitment professionals	**1** Ask for introductions via my current network **2** Look at job boards specialising in HR roles	**1** Fortnightly phone call or email **2** Connect on LinkedIn **3** Follow on Twitter (if they tweet)
HR and L&D directors, plus HR professionals generally	**1** Attend CIPD events and conferences **2** Ask for introductions via my current network **3** Join LinkedIn groups with HR professionals **4** Answer LinkedIn questions on leadership **5** Blog at training zone and HR zone	**1** Connect on LinkedIn **2** Comment on blogs about leadership issues **3** Link my blog to my LinkedIn profile and post in my LinkedIn groups **4** Ask for a phone call or meeting

Very often you will find that you start to have a daily, weekly and monthly networking routine in order to implement your networking strategy and networking plan. It can be helpful to write down what this routine is and diarise your actions (see Figure 15.1 for an example).

DAILY NETWORKING ROUTINE

- Check my 'people to keep close to' list and @ mentions on Twitter
- Do my 9-min daily LinkedIn routine

WEEKLY NETWORKING ROUTINE

- Attend fortnightly breakfast meeting
- Add new blog post to Defero Law
- Check prominent legal bloggers and comment on at least one new blog post
- Find 20–30 articles to share on Twitter & LinkedIn for the next week

MONTHLY NETWORKING ROUTINE

- Update my relationship plans and plan activity for next 3 months
- Plan my blogging content for the next week

---

figure 15.1 Example of a networking routine

Making yourself accountable

> **You need someone to keep you accountable to your goals**

For goals to be achieved routinely, you need someone to keep you accountable to your goals. If you are in employment, this is very likely to be your line manager. If you are self-employed or looking for a new job, who can you use to keep you accountable to your networking action plan? Perhaps a partner, relative or good friend?

Summary

A plan turns your strategy into actions.

People's networking goals and preferences are very personal, and not every group, event or online networking site will suit everyone or be effective for everyone. Take the time to assess and research what are the best places for you personally to network to achieve your goal.

To harness the power of both face-to-face and online networking, decide which tools and processes you will use to strengthen the relationships that matter to you.

ACTION POINTS

■ Calculate your networking opportunity score. What are three actions you could do to improve your opportunity score in order to help you achieve your networking goals?

■ Find two different online networking sites that could help you meet potential A-listers.

■ Look at your list of A-listers. Analyse the state of your relationship with each of them, and put in place an action plan to improve the level of the relationship with each of them.

■ Ask two of your peers which, in their view, are the best local networking events and groups.

■ Attend two new events or networking groups as a guest.

■ Brainstorm tools and processes to strengthen relationships and maintain contact with your network. Make sure you include online and face-to-face tools and processes.

■ Write your networking action plan, which will help you achieve your networking goal(s). Find someone to share your networking action plan with.

Further resources

Books

Ferrazzi, K., *Never Eat Alone: And other secrets to success, one relationship at a time*, Crown Business, 2005 (expected updated 2nd edn June 2014).

Misner, I. and Donovan, M.R., *The 29% Solution*, Olive Tree Press, 2008.

Tracy, B., *Eat That Frog! Get more of the important things done – today!*, Berrett-Koehler Hodder Paperbacks, Jan. 2013.

Websites

Joined Up Networking www.joinedupnetworking.com for worksheets to help you:

■ calculate your networking opportunity score

■ brainstorm ways to increase your networking opportunity score

■ identify tools and processes to strengthen the relationships in your network.

16

How to fit it all in

What topics are covered in this chapter?

▦ Practical tips and techniques to be able to communicate with your network in a time-efficient manner

As you were reading through the book, I am sure you were thinking at various points, 'But how am I going to make the time to do all of this?' This chapter will show you how to use your networking time wisely and make your network work for you rather than the other way round.

Be realistic with your time

Free time is the one thing that most professionals, managers or business owners don't have. But to be successful at networking, you need to commit time to growing and maintaining your network. So, before you agree to attend lots of networking groups and maintain a highly visible presence on a range of online networking sites and tools, you need to be realistic about what time you have available for networking. For example, if you want to join a referral generation club and maximise your chances of generating referrals from club members, then you need to begin with the intention to have a one-to-one meeting with every single member of the club within the first couple of months of joining. Say, for example, the club has 20 members; once you include your travelling time and research, that's a minimum time commitment of 30+ hours. However, in reality, you will be able to prioritise who you should meet first. If you join an online forum to

❝You need to commit time to growing and maintaining your network❞

generate business, you need to be prepared to visit and comment on that forum every single day.

As a general rule of thumb, unless you need to repurpose your network, you want to be spending at least 70 per cent of your networking time maintaining and strengthening relationships within your current network.

Take a look at the vacant times in your diary – how much time, realistically, do you have to allocate to networking?

Experiment and measure results

A powerful networking strategy always will contain a mixture of ways to meet and keep in touch with people. As networking results are not a linear cause-and-effect relationship, not every group, event or forum will yield the results you require. Over time you will find out that some groups, events and relationships have a better rate of return: potential A-listers will turn out to be C-listers, whereas a C-lister may turn out to be a useful B-lister or A-lister. (For a definition of what makes an A-, B- or C-lister, see Chapter 7.) For example, I think of my next-door neighbour, who works for the local fire service, as a good friend, but, in networking terms, I class her as a C-lister. A week after I had told her that I was writing this book, she introduced me to someone who engaged me for some work. The moral of this story is always to leave open the communication channels between yourself and the C-listers within your network.

To make sure that you are investing your time in networking wisely, experiment with new groups and events, but regularly measure your results and progress so that you can see where or with whom to spend more time or less time to generate better results.

When you measure your results, you can then fine-tune how much networking time you need to spend monthly to generate the level of results you require. For example, Bryony Thomas knows that she needs to meet ten people physically when networking each month to generate a healthy flow of new business.

Block out time in your diary

Follow-up and maintenance of a relationship takes time. The best way to follow up efficiently is to do what Karen Spillane does – she dedicates 30 minutes each day to following up and communicating with her network. Robert Watson, coach to authors, allocates two 30-minute periods each week, starting at 11:30 am, to follow up with his network. He chooses this time, as it gives him a break from his morning work and helps him wind down to lunch. More importantly, Robert has found that many of his network are around at their desks and prepared to take a phone call at 11:30 am.

Block out time weekly and monthly in your diary to plan your networking time and activities. Use this time to prioritise who you need to meet and why.

Delegate

You can delegate some of your networking tasks to a personal or virtual assistant. For example, they can research:

▓ people for you to meet

▓ groups and events for you to attend

▓ interesting content for you to write about or share.

As well as helping you with your research, they can take on some of the routine admin tasks, such as:

▓ diary and meeting management

▓ follow-up emails

▓ entering contact details from business cards into your CRM software

▓ running reports from your CRM software

▓ updating your social media profiles

▓ posting your articles on blog sites.

Automate

Many networkers fall into the trap of thinking that they have to do everything themselves. There are many tools available to the networker that help to save time, such as the following.

RSS feed readers

Use these to 'read' all the important blogs and forum posts in one place.

Search alerts

These are web-based services that alert you whenever content is created that contains a keyword that is important to you, such as your name.

Client relationship management software

This is a type of software that helps you manage your relationships and keep track of your conversations with your contacts. Some of these systems will allow you to connect with your contacts' social media profiles, so you can see all of your network's social media activity from one place. Most of these types of software will allow you to categorise all your contacts by adding tags. I recommend that you use the following tags to manage your network effectively:

Relationship level: 1 to 5

Importance to you: A-, B- or C-lister

With these tags you can run reports to help you prioritise who you need to spend time with. For example, you want to aim to have all your A-listers at a relationship level of 4 – *collaborate* – or 5 – *inner circle*.

Twitter and LinkedIn third-party applications

Use these often free pieces of software to benefit more effectively from Twitter and LinkedIn. For example, there are applications that let you:

- see just the tweets that matter to you, e.g. Tweetdeck and Hootsuite
- publish new posts from your blog to your social networking accounts, e.g. Twitterfeed
- find people to follow and unfollow
- find lists of people important to you
- do keyword searches on Twitter
- upload pictures and videos
- do many other things, too.

Blog plugins

These are little pieces of coding that help you get more functionality from your blog. For example, these can:

■ connect your blog to Twitter

■ optimise your blog for Google search engine rankings

■ allow people to sign up for your newsletter from your blog

■ stop spam comment protection

■ do many other things, too.

Be discerning

Your time is precious, and networking takes time. Possibly the biggest time-wasting habit many networkers have is spending time meeting or maintaining relationships with the wrong type of people. Only you will know who you need to meet – however, it takes discipline and focus to leave a group, event or conversation that is not going to help you achieve your results. Get into the habit of routinely evaluating your conversations as you are having them – and always ask yourself, is this person or conversation going to help me achieve my goals? If the answer is 'No', then politely move on.

Spend time developing your networking skills

Networking, both face-to-face and online, is a skill that everyone can develop. Sadly, many professionals just jump in at the deep end when networking and don't take the time to attend any networking training, or even hone their networking skills by reading a book like this.

Do invest your time to undergo some personal development on networking. Far from being a sign of weakness, it is actually a sign that you are serious about your business and career success. Sometimes it's the small changes, such as how you introduce yourself, that actually have the biggest impact.

Look after your A-listers

'One good advocate is worth ten clients.'

Richard White, The Accidental Salesman® and author of The Accidental
Salesman®: Networking survival guide[1]

Your A-listers are your word-of-mouth marketing team. These are your
unpaid sales force. As they are 'unpaid', they have to *want* to recommend
you. Therefore, it is worth focusing your networking time on these people
and looking after them as much as possible. Who can you introduce
them to? How can you help them in their role?
For example, one of my inner circle and A-listers is
David Stoch, who runs Meerkat PR. He is very good
at giving me a phone call fortnightly, in addition
to the tweets we routinely exchange, to keep the
relationship warm and mutually beneficial.

**❝Your A-listers
are your word-of-
mouth marketing
team❞**

Network whilst you eat

Everyone needs to eat. When I was employed I used to use my lunch
times to meet people in my network. Grabbing a coffee or a sandwich
with someone you really want to meet can be an easy way to get a
meeting with someone. How about inviting a few of your network for a
meal? That way, they get to make new connections, you gain precious
social capital but, more importantly, you have been able to spend high-
quality face-to-face time with several members of your network at the
same time.

> **Tip**
>
> When meeting someone over lunch or dinner, order less than you would normally.
> This will allow you more time to talk and engage in conversation.

Do you need a face-to-face meeting?

When you add in travelling time, face-to-face meetings are a large investment from you. Before I meet someone face-to-face normally I will have a
phone or video-conference meeting with them. Only if, during this initial

---

[1] White, R., *The Accidental Salesman®: Networking survival guide*, Book Shaker, 2011.

discussion, I see the potential for collaboration or a potential A-lister for me, will I then commit to a face-to-face meeting.

Keep the content on your online networking sites fresh

'The days when you would do a formal introduction on meeting someone new are now long gone. People have already checked you out on social media.'

Keith Robinson, Launchpad Recruits

Get into the habit of updating your status on your online networking sites regularly. This is an easy and quick way of keeping in touch with many of your network at once. Often I find that my status updates will prompt a conversation with one of my network.

Summary

Allocate time each week to networking. Put in place a process or system to help you maintain contact with your existing A-listers. Then spend some time finding and meeting up with new A-listers.

Wherever possible, delegate or automate the admin tasks to free up your time.

ACTION POINTS

▧ Plan 30 minutes a day in your diary to help you keep in contact with your network.

▧ Identify three tasks to help you maintain your network that you could delegate or automate.

▧ Next time you are in an unproductive conversation at a networking event, have a go at withdrawing politely from the conversation.

▧ Think who you could ask to join you for lunch next week. Now go and book your lunch date.

▧ Plan a networking lunch or dinner with three other people within your network who you think would benefit from knowing each other.

▧ Find three different ways in which you could help A-listers within your network this week.

▧ Commit to updating your Facebook and LinkedIn status every day for a month. Notice how many more conversations this prompts with your network.

Further resources

Books

Covey, S., *The 7 Habits of Highly Effective People*, Simon & Schuster, 2004.

Ferrazzi, K., *Never Eat Alone: And other secrets to success, one relationship at a time*, Crown Business, 2005 (expected updated 2nd edn June 2014).

Websites

Joined Up Networking www.joinedupnetworking.com

17

A final word about networking

The relentless pace of developments in communications technology is rapidly changing how people interact across geographical and cultural boundaries. It's pretty much a given, in this internet-enabled age, that future success will come easily to those savvy professionals and business owners who have worked out who they need to know *and* how to easily get found by others. For these people, their network has become intrinsic to their current and future business success. It's this network that will provide them with the answers, guidance and opportunities needed to get ahead in business.

If you want to be one of those people, it all comes down to answering and acting proactively on the answers to these three simple questions about your network:

- Who do you need to add into your network?
- Where do you meet them?
- How do you maintain and strengthen the relationships?

No employer or competitor can ever take your network away from you

Your network is your own, and something that will accompany you as you go through life. No employer or competitor can ever take your network away from you. It's a personal asset which, if invested in, will yield a rate of return far greater than any other form of activity, process or system.

Whether you realise it or not, you are networking every time you start a conversation. You have a choice – how will you use those conversations?

Will you actively look to build relationships with people in a position to help you generate career and business success?

Or will you carry on as before...?

Appendix 1

Useful *Financial Times* articles

Networking becomes a dirty word

By Neil Bearden

MBA students need to view their contacts as people rather than things

The brains of business school students around the world have been infected with a dirty word: network. They are repeatedly told that their "network" is one of their most important assets. Sometimes they are led to believe that their networks are even more important than their courses.

The problem, I believe, is that the network metaphor carries the wrong connotations. The word encourages business school students to view their so-called network as a group of interconnected things, rather than a group of people. Moreover this focus, or perhaps even tunnel vision, on their network encourages MBA students to behave badly and on occasion rudely.

Individuals naturally speak in metaphors. But although often useful as thinking aids, metaphors can also become thinking traps.

MBA students are told: "It is very important that you grow your network. It will be one of your greatest assets in your career." Depending on how this advice is interpreted, MBA students may begin to view others as plants or maybe even as a stack of poker chips. Either interpretation is a trap.

Using the metaphor of the plant, many seeds have to be sown and an MBA cohort becomes a kind of garden. Promising plants need to be watered regularly and less promising ones – the weeds – should be discarded. On the other hand, when MBA students view people as poker chips they try to gather as many of these chips as possible. The number of Facebook friends and the number of LinkedIn connections determines the value of an MBA's network. The person with the largest stack wins.

But people in networks cannot be compared with plants or poker chips, they are people. One does not need to be an emotional genius to know that when people are treated like plants or poker chips they do not appreciate it. Yet many MBAs – so entranced by their network metaphor – appear unaware of this obvious fact.

As a business school professor I come in contact with many MBA students each year. By the chip metric I am in the World Series on LinkedIn, although I have sent fewer than 20 connect requests myself. I receive a lot of requests to connect and then a lot of subsequent requests for other things. Current and former students ask for technical help, for me to connect them with people in a company they would like to work for and so on. That is fine. What is not fine is that I receive thanks for the help I give less than half the time I provide it.

I have asked other professors and also working professionals whether they receive any thanks and most say that too often they do not. A typical scenario runs like this: an individual working in a bank receives an email from an MBA student begging for a coffee chat. They meet and the student gets the advice he or she wants. The banker pays for the coffee and then never hears from the student again.

I hear similar stories from social entrepreneurs, consultants and people working in industry. They are tired of ungrateful MBAs and many have decided to stop responding to requests for help. They do not want to be treated like a network node; they want to be respected for who they are: people.

The antidote to this virus is simple: business school administrators and professors should stop telling students to grow their networks. Instead they should tell them to develop their relationships and to treat people with the respect they deserve. When people feel respected, they like to provide help and support. When they feel manipulated like a tool, they do not.

Immanuel Kant has some great advice that could be applied to MBA students: "Act in such a way that you treat humanity, whether in your own person or in that of another, always at the same time as an end and never merely as a means."

The author is associate professor of decision sciences, Insead.

Source: Bearden, N., 'Networking becomes a dirty word', *Financial Times*, 2 February 2014.
© Neil Bearden 2014.

Putting a price on your contacts

By Maija Palmer

When Boardex started mapping the professional relationships between prominent business people, the London-based company was targeting corporate governance watchdogs as clients.

James Daly, chief executive, thought its database would be used to track connections between executives and board members to guard against cronyism in the wake of Enron's 2001 collapse.

The product eventually took off – but not in the way Boardex intended. Corporate governance watchdogs were interested, "but they didn't have the budget to spend on it".

Instead, the database was picked up by bankers and lawyers as a way of identifying which employees were best placed to win new business.

Mr Daly says clients are paying up to $1m a year to use the data. "Two years ago it started to become a trend. Companies started looking at the relationships their employees had and recognised it as a form of capital."

Technology such as Boardex's is indeed making it easier to put a value on the adage "it is not what you know, it is who you know", both for high-level employees and rank-and-file workers.

In recent years, for instance, companies such as Klout, Kred and Peer-Index have emerged, promising to measure the level of influence that an individual has online.

Factors such as how many followers someone has on Twitter and how influential those followers are can be condensed into a single number by Klout. Accenture, the consultant, is among those using it as part of its recruitment process in the US.

Profiles on the LinkedIn networking service are another guide to an individual's connectedness, publicly listing how many contacts someone has (although it stops counting at 500).

But to what extent should employers track such indicators when they hire, promote and manage staff?

Michael Wright, head of talent acquisition for the Asia Pacific region for Group M, an advertising company, says that, while he would never hire someone solely on the basis of their Klout score or LinkedIn profile, it can be a useful filter for weeding out candidates.

"If someone has just four connections on LinkedIn and they haven't bothered to upload a photo, it is a warning sign. They would be off our long list of candidates for a role," he says.

"If someone is looking to relocate from Europe to Asia and a quick scan through their contacts shows they have no connections in Asia, that would count against them as this is a relationship business," he adds.

Paul Guely, managing partner at Arma Partners, a corporate finance advisory firm, says technical tools can only be a small part of the process.

He says: "I am a member of a number of social networks and I do get value from them in terms of seeing who knows who. But when I want to understand what 'know' means – whether someone trusts this person, how much business they really do together – I have not yet found a substitute for the off-the-record phone call to someone who knows them."

Russell Reynolds, an executive search firm, is one of the more than 250 companies that use Boardex's software. Tim Cook, co-leader of its information officers practice, finds the software useful for looking at a candidate's job history, but says it can never be a complete substitute for a recruiter's own market insight.

"Knowing who is connected to who is interesting, but knowing who has excelled in their role and how they have done it is the insight on which we act," he says.

The Boardex database maps relationships between more than 600,000 business people. If a bank wants to pitch to a company for work – to Intel, say – the software can indicate which of its employees are closest to Intel senior management.

The relationships are ranked by strength, "so that having met someone once at a cocktail party does not have the same value as having served on a board with them for 10 years," Mr Daly says.

The most valuable information is not so much the direct connections, which might be known through other means, but the second-degree ones, which are more difficult to discover.

The system can also show a company areas where it lacks connections, as well as the impact a particular employee's departure might have.

Mr Daly goes so far as to claim that its algorithms could put an overall financial value on a company's relationships that would merit being placed on its balance sheet alongside other intangible assets. He believes such a number would be at least as valid as an estimate of goodwill – a notoriously finger-in-the-air asset created in takeovers.

But even as companies are offered new ways to value their employees' relationships, there is concern in some cases over who owns those networks. Put bluntly: are your business contacts your own or the company's?

Mr Daly talks of a "healthy tension" between individuals and their employers on this point. This is by no means entirely new. The loss of valuable connections has always been a threat to any relationship-based business, such as investment banking.

The tension is also creeping into the world of social media, however; courts have yet to work out a clear position on who owns what online when an employee leaves.

Donna Ballman, an employment lawyer and author of the book *Stand Up For Yourself Without Getting Fired*, says that as "relationship capital" becomes more important, employment contracts will need to start including more clauses on ownership of online networks.

"This issue continues to be a hot topic in employment law. The courts frequently look to what the parties agreed in any contracts. I see provisions dealing with social media in employment agreements, confidentiality agreements, intellectual property agreements and non-solicitation agreements," she says.

Even so, it remains unclear whether such contracts related to social media can be enforced. If any of the contacts are deemed to be in the public domain, for example, ownership clauses would not apply.

So how worried should you be if your own Klout score is less than stellar and you do not have a contact who knows Larry Ellison and can therefore make you stand out on the Boardex database?

"It is just one tool in a very big toolbox," says Mr Wright, of Group M. "The final decision on hiring needs human assessment. But it will be used more and more. I have a friend who says you are the product of the people you keep company with and I think there is some truth in that."

Online poaching by former staff

Companies are used to clashing with former employees that try to poach clients or otherwise exploit professional relationships they had nurtured in their old role.

The rise of social media, however, has created fresh potential for conflict when well-connected employees quit. The question increasingly being raised is: who gets to exploit the departing worker's online network?

So far, the case law in this area is mixed.

Litigation in the US between PhoneDog, a mobile phone review site, and one of its former employees, Noah Kravitz, was expected to be a test case last year.

Mr Kravitz had created a Twitter account, @PhoneDog_Noah, which he used to promote the company, gaining 17,000 followers in the process.

When he left the company he changed the Twitter handle to @noahkravitz but retained the 17,000 followers.

PhoneDog sued him for $340,000, putting a price of $2.50 on each Twitter follower, per month. However, the case was settled out of court and although Mr Kravitz did keep his followers, it is unclear whether he paid for them.

Naked bosses and other gym hazards

By Rhymer Rigby

In his 2012 "quit 'n' tell" book, *Why I Left Goldman Sachs*, Greg Smith detailed some of things he had seen in the company gym, such as the "impressive weight" Hank Paulson put on the incline chest-press machine. Most notable, though, was his description of Lloyd Blankfein "walking around the changing room au naturel to dry off from his shower". Charitably, Mr Smith went on to add that this kind of air-drying was "not uncommon among a generation slightly older than mine".

Clearly, these are words of a man who had burnt his bridges. But they do raise some interesting questions. How should you react to colleagues in the gym? Is it good form to thrash your boss at squash? And what do you say to a naked boss?

For starters, it is worth remembering that a gym is a public space. Moreover, there is a kind of general etiquette with rules that range from not letting eyes linger on others to wiping sweat off machines. However, says Nic Hammarling, head of diversity at business psychologists Pearn Kandola, "it is naive to think that the world of work and the gym are entirely separate".

On a positive note, Ms Hammarling says that going to the gym can help your career prospects as it breaks down traditional boundaries and builds commonality and trust: "It can be a good place to meet more senior people and those from other parts of the organisation and do some informal networking."

Etiquette consultant Jodi RR Smith adds that the gym may even help you to connect with those with whom you normally struggle to form bonds.

Personal trainer Kathryn Freeland notes there may be benefits for your workout too: "If you're the kind of person who tends to slack off and play with your smartphone, seeing your boss in the gym could make you work out harder."

On the competitive side of things, you should avoid losing on purpose to suck up to a boss. "One of the worst ways to build relationships is underplay your strengths as they'll realise and it damages trust," says Ms Hammarling. However, you also need to be aware of the kind of person your boss is – and, if they are a poor sport, you might avoid overt competition with them.

For many gym-goers, though, the elephant in the changing room is managerial nudity. Ms Smith says that while saying hello is rarely a problem, "the bigger question is what to do if the naked boss starts a full-blown conversation". If you are uncomfortable here, she advises you could point out they're discussing business publicly: "Make it about the confidentiality, not the nakedness. Or, if the changing room is empty, say: 'Let me grab my towel.'"

You should, of course, avoid sharing these encounters with colleagues, amusing though they may be. "What happens at the gym stays at the gym," says Ms Smith.

If I was ... wanting to switch careers

By Rachel B. Polhemus

Rachel Polhemus is senior partner at Witt/Kieffer, an executive search firm specialising in healthcare, education and not-for-profit organisations. Here, she puts herself in the position of someone seeking to switch careers:

It seems there is no such thing as a stable, predictable career any more. Individuals rarely stick with the same employer, much less the same industry or even profession.

I work with a lot of senior executives who for one reason or another – midlife crisis, a recent lay-off, a desire to make a difference – find themselves looking for a new career challenge.

If I found myself in that position, I would hope to be one of the lucky few who have new opportunities handed to them on a platter. But if not, I would set about rethinking my skills, goals, values and mindset – in marketing language, I would be "repositioning my brand".

Here are strategies I would use:

First, I would develop a personal mission statement. What is it that I want and value? Can I express it to myself and others? Committing a mission statement to paper will guide every future decision.

Knowing my values will be vital. It is easy to say "I want something more" but harder for me to recognise the factors that truly trigger my career motivation and happiness. Knowing my values will allow me to project which new career opportunity is a "good fit", even if it seems like a sideways – or even downward – move.

Similarly, I need to know my skills. A surprising number of successful professionals cannot express what has made them successful. I therefore want to know what I do best, and what my limitations are.

I would ask colleagues and confidants and use objective skills and personality assessment tools. This will tell me which skills are transferable to other careers – and which might inhibit transformation.

I would also be active in volunteer organisations, professional groups, boards of directors, and fundraisers. These activities should give me important feedback, introduce me to different people, and lead me along paths I might never otherwise have found.

As a rule of thumb, two-thirds of job opportunities come from networking, so I would want to network well. I would make sure I am "real" and not just seeing what I can get out of each meeting or email. Overdoing it, by talking about myself and promoting my brand too much, might look disrespectful or desperate.

I would engage with people, enjoy them for their wisdom and insight, and share my experiences as well. This will leave a meaningful impression and get me remembered – and recommended.

Many mid to late-career executives are hesitant to try new ways of connecting with peers, for example via LinkedIn groups, or attending a new conference.

But I would remember that new forms of networking can put me in touch with dynamic professionals.

While it will be important to engage with new people in new ways, I will also re-engage with my traditional contacts. Those who have made big career changes might offer tips and leads.

Recruiters and executive search consultants can help and I would seek their objective advice and support – but only after completing the strategies above.

Repositioning a career is not easy, but if my gut tells me it's right, then it probably is. I will be doing something many professionals and executives dream about but never act upon.

Source: Polhemus, R.B., 'If I was ... wanting to switch careers', *Financial Times*, 12 February 2014.
© Rachel B. Polhemus 2014.

The importance of bridging the cultural divide

By Rebecca Knight

As a graduate student in the late 1990s, Andy Molinsky worked at an agency in Boston helping Russian immigrants find jobs in the US. The applicants were well-qualified but they struggled during interviews.

They intellectually understood the cultural customs of the typical US job interview – smile, make eye contact and engage in small talk – but they found it hard to do so because it went against their culturally ingrained behaviour.

Now an associate professor of organisational behaviour at Brandeis International Business School, Massachusetts, Prof Molinsky was motivated to learn more about overcoming the challenges of cultural identity in the workplace. His book *Global Dexterity* (Harvard Business School Press) aims to help managers learn how to culturally code-switch when working in an international setting.

What is global dexterity?

It's the ability to adapt your behaviour across cultures without losing yourself in the process – fitting in without giving in. When you're making your way in an international culture you will find yourself in situations where how you would act in your native culture is different from the way you are expected to act in your new culture. This could range from how you pitch yourself to an investor, to how you motivate employees, to how you give performance feedback.

Why is global dexterity a "critical skill" for today's managers?

Everything you need to do in order to do your job well has the potential to vary across cultures. So you need the ability to not only diagnose and understand these differences but also to be able to shift and adjust your behaviour accordingly. If you don't, you risk being ineffective: you won't be able to achieve your goals or the goals of the business.

Give an example

Take one of my MBA students from Beijing going to a networking event on campus with potential employers. He is aware of the US-style assertiveness and self-promotional behaviour necessary. He knows that Americans openly tout their skills and accomplishments and are less deferential to potential employers. But for the Beijing student the real challenge is adapting his behaviour because it goes against the notions of power and respect ingrained in him since he was a kid. Some international students have told me they avoid going to career fairs because it's so uncomfortable for them.

How do you master global dexterity?

It's about customising a style that works for you. Sometimes it requires eliminating certain behaviours, other times it can be something as small as a linguistic change. For example, in Russia, consulting firms are very hierarchical. You don't necessarily vie for projects – you're slotted into them. One Russian student realised her US colleagues were advocating for themselves and she was losing out on the best work. But telling her boss, "I'd love to work on this project", felt too difficult for her. Her solution was to customise her language and ask: "Can I be helpful on this project?".

Are some better at this than others?

There are some people who are naturally more socially skilled and attuned to social and cultural cues. But there are many individuals who aren't able to do that as easily. I strongly believe anyone can learn this stuff. It's a skill; there's no global dexterity gene.

Are business schools missing an opportunity here?

A lot of business schools do short-term immersion trips and have this idea that: "We are global. We send you abroad. By osmosis you'll learn from people of other cultures." This is a nice first step but it doesn't equip people to be effective global leaders. There's no framework or tools. We need to sensitise people to these issues.

MBA gender gap: tips on networking

By Charlotte Clarke

Polly McMaster is an MBA graduate of London Business School and chief executive of The Fold, an online fashion business specialising in professional clothing for women. Her five top tips on networking are:

1. Be creative – remember your network can be drawn from all areas of your life: your family, friends, school and university and all the jobs you might have had. Don't be afraid to reach out to them in a professional manner – if they are friends they are even more likely to help you.

2. Know your industry – networking is a fundamental part of growing your career, especially at senior levels. Once you become the one on the team responsible for generating business, you need to have a network to call on. It is therefore really important to go to events with your industry, make friends with your peers and if you have the chance to go to business school that will generate a step-change in your network.

3. Don't be shy – when at a conference or networking event don't hesitate about going up to people. Or if you are in a group and you see someone on their own, invite them to join. The best networking events can be those which have a focus or activity – that way you can meet new people more easily rather than just standing in a room and being forced to step into a new conversation.

4. Go solo – it is tempting to go to conferences or events with a friend or colleague. If you do that, make sure that you don't just talk to each other through the event, it's a comfortable fall back option but won't encourage you to meet new people.

5. Dress for success – standing out with what you wear can be a great conversation starter. Go for a bright colour, bold necklace or interesting dress. You'll be surprised how many "I love your dress/necklace/jacket" comments will then lead to a new contact.

Source: Clarke, C., 'MBA gender gap: tips on networking', *Financial Times*, 19 November 2013.

Glossary

4Networking or **4N** a UK-based networking organisation that has groups that meet all over the UK, as well as an active online forum.

40- or **60-second pitch** another name for the short pitch, which many networking groups require each member to deliver each time they meet.

A-lister someone who is well connected to your target market and an advocate for your services.

App a piece of software commonly found on smart phones that is used to give additional functionality to the hardware device.

Athena a women-only networking group.

Avatar the picture of a member that online networking sites display.

Bing Microsoft's search engine.

Blog or **weblog** an online journal based on the web.

Blogger someone who hosts or writes a blog, as well as a popular piece of blogging software.

Blogging the practice of writing a blog.

Blogosphere a term used to describe blogs on the internet.

BNI the largest referral generation organisation in the world. Most referral generation clubs are based on BNI in some way.

Business card a small, wallet-sized piece of card with a person's contact details on.

Business for Breakfast or **B4B** a franchise-based referral generation club in the UK.

Conversation thread the continuing conversation or discussion on an internet forum.

CPD (Continuing Professional Development) points – some professional institutes require their members to record and complete a certain number of CPD hours or points.

Credibility your ability to walk your walk, talk your talk, and deliver on your commitments.

DM (direct message) a way of sending private messages between users on Twitter.

Drupal blogging software.

Elevator pitch term used for the short sales pitch that networkers often are asked to deliver at networking events.

Facebook the largest social network in the world.

Feedburner a service provided by Google that allows people to subscribe easily to your blog in a medium that suits them, e.g. via RSS or email.

Flaming the act of inciting an argument on a social networking site.

Google the world's most popular search engine.

Google+ Google's social networking platform.

Guest speaker many networking events use a guest speaker as a focal point of the event.

Hiring manager the individual in a company or organisation responsible for hiring a new member of staff.

Jelly groups groups where freelancers and self-employed people meet up to work together.

Joined-up networking the practice of using both online and face-to-face networking for greater business and career success.

Lead a potential enquiry or opportunity to gain business.

LinkedIn a social networking site frequented by professionals. It has been called the professional's version of Facebook.

LinkedIn groups private and public communities on LinkedIn.

Mastermind group a group of people who meet regularly to give each other peer-to-peer mentoring and support.

Micro-blogging a form of blogging where users are limited to being able to post only short messages. Twitter probably is the best known form of micro-blogging.

Monthly minute another name for an elevator pitch.

MySpace social networking site focused on music.

Ning a piece of software that allows people to have their own social networking site.

Non-executive or **non-exec. experience** a mastermind group.

Online forums websites where registered users can post discussions or contribute to discussions by replying to the original post.

Online networking the practice of meeting people via the internet.

Online profile or **biography** an introduction to you that most online networking sites ask every user to fill out.

Original poster or **OP** the person who starts a discussion on an online forum.

PageRank a weighting Google gives each website, which determines how frequently it returns to each site to see if any content has changed. The higher the page rank, the more visits from Google.

Peeps or **tweeters** what people on Twitter call themselves.

Personal branding what people say about you when you are out of the room.

Pinterest a social networking site focused on sharing images.

Plaxo an online address book site.

Plugin a piece of coding that 'plugs' into a piece of software to give it additional functionality. Used extensively with open source software, such as WordPress.

PM a private message on a social networking site.

Post an entry in an online forum or blog.

Profession lock-out policy the practice of allowing only one type of a certain profession in a networking group, e.g. only one accountant is allowed within the group.

Referral when one of your network passes you an opportunity.

Referral generation group/club a group of people who have joined together to help each other generate referrals for the wider group.

Retweet or **RT** when people on Twitter share someone's tweet with all their followers.

RSS (Really Simple Syndication) feed a way of easily updating people interested in your site when it changes.

RSS reader a piece of software that allows you to read RSS feeds in one place.

Skype™ a service that allows users to make free video or audio calls over the internet to other Skype users.

Slideshare a site where users can share their presentations.

Smartphone a phone that (as well as taking phone calls) can access the internet.

SMS (short message service) normally used to send text messages or text-based chat conversations.

Social bookmarking a type of social networking site where users on the site share bookmarks to websites.

Social capital the imaginary emotional bank account that you build up by being helpful to people.

Social media a collection of data, photos and video assembled by users.

Social networking websites that allow users to group together in communities.

Spammer someone who sends you unsolicited messages about their products.

Speed networking a form of networking where participants have a short, timed conversation before moving on to talk to someone else at the event.

Status updates functionality on a social networking site that allows users to post messages about their status.

Sub short for substitute. Members at a referral group often are required to send a substitute if they cannot attend a meeting.

Teleseminar a form of seminar where participants join in over the telephone.

Troll a term for someone who deliberately posts negative or highly critical comments, blogs or posts.

Tweet a message on Twitter, which is limited to 140 characters.

Tweeters what people on Twitter call themselves.

Tweeting the practice of using Twitter to send messages.

Twitter a micro-blogging service that limits users to posts of a maximum of 140 characters.

Twitter lists a function on Twitter where users can group together followers.

Twitterati highly influential and often visible users of Twitter.

URL the address of a web page.

URL shortening service a service that allows you to shorten addresses of web pages – vital if you are limited to only 140 characters in your updates.

User profiles information about you entered into a social networking site.

Virtual boardroom a mastermind group.

VOIP (Voice Over Internet Protocol) telephony services that are provided over the internet. Perhaps the best known VOIP service is Skype.

Webinar a form of seminar where listeners join in over the web.

Weblog the first name and form of blogs.

WiBN Women in Business Network.

WordPress an open source piece of blogging software.

Working the room a phrase that describes the practice of finding people to talk to in a room full of strangers.

Xing a social networking site.

Yahoo a search engine, email provider and news site.

Yammer a private micro-blogging site. An 'in-house' version of Twitter.

YouTube a video-sharing site and the second biggest search engine after Google.

Further resources

Books

Networking and relationship building

Benjamin, S., *Perfect Phrases for Professional Networking*, McGraw-Hill Professional, 2009.

Bolles, R.N., *What Color is Your Parachute?* Ten Speed Press, 2008.

Bounds, A., *The Jelly Effect: How to make your communications stick*, Capstone, 2010.

Burton, B., *Get Off Your Arse*, 4Publishing, 2009.

Covey, S., *The 7 Habits of Highly Effective People*, Simon & Schuster, 2004.

D'Souza, S., *Brilliant Networking: What the best networkers know, do and say*, 2nd edition, Prentice Hall, 2010.

Ferrazzi, K., *Never Eat Alone: And other secrets to success, one relationship at a time*, Crown Business, 2005 (expected updated 2nd edn June 2014).

Frankel, L., *Nice Girls Don't Get the Corner Office*, Little, Brown & Company, 2004.

Lindenfield, G. and Lindenfield, S., *Confident Networking for Career Success and Satisfaction*, Piatkus Books, 2005.

Lopata A. and Roper, P., *...And Death Came Third! The definitive guide to networking and speaking in public*, Book Shaker, 2006.

Lopata, A., *Recommended: The ultimate masterclass in selling through referrals and networking*, Financial Times Prentice Hall, 2011.

Misner, I.R., Alexander, D.C. and Hilliard, B., *Networking Like a Pro: Turning contacts into connections*, Entrepreneur Press, 2010.

Misner, I.R. and Donovan, M.R., *The 29% Solution*, Olive Tree Press, 2008.

Thomas, S., *Professional Networking for Dummies*, John Wiley & Sons, 2014.

Tracy, B., *Eat That Frog! Get more of the important things done – today!* Berrett-Koehler Publishers, 2002.

White, R., *The Accidental Salesman®: Networking survival guide – the essential hands-on manual for winning more business and gaining new sales lead*s, Book Shaker, 2011.

Social media and online networking

Brogan, C., *Social Media 101: Tactics and tips to develop your business online*, John Wiley & Sons, 2010.

Brogan, C. and Smith, J., *Trust Agents: Using the web to build influence, improve reputation and earn trust, revised edition*, John Wiley & Sons, 2010.

Clapperton, G., *This is Social Media: Tweet, blog, link and post your way to business success*, Capstone, 2009.

Halligan, B. and Shah, D., *Inbound Marketing: Get found using Google, social media and blogs*, John Wiley & Sons, 2009.

Qualman, E., *Socialnomics: How social media transforms the way we live and do business*, 2nd edition, John Wiley & Sons, 2010.

Reed, J., *Get up to Speed with Online Marketing: How to use websites, blogs, social networking and much more*, Financial Times Prentice Hall, 2010.

Blogging

Rowse, D. and Garrett, C., *ProBlogger: Secrets for blogging your way to a six-figure income*, 2nd edition, John Wiley & Sons, 2010.

Thewlis, P., *WordPress for Business Bloggers*, Packt Publishing, 2008.

Building an online community

Bernoff, J. and Li, C., *Groundswell*, Harvard Business School Press, 2008.

O'Keefe, P., *Managing Online Forums*, Amacom, 2008.

Personal branding

Schawbel, D., *Me 2.0: Build a powerful brand to achieve career success*, revised edition, Kaplan Trade, 2010.

Social capital

Cialdini, R., *Influence: The psychology of persuasion*, revised edition, 1st Collins Business Essentials, 2007.

Gladwell, M., *The Tipping Point*, Abacus, 2001.

Cultural diversity

Morrison, T. and Conaway, W.A., *Kiss, Bow or Shake Hands*, Adams Media Corporation, 2006.

Trompenaars, F. and Hampden-Turner, C., *Riding the Waves of Culture: Understanding cultural diversity in business*, Nicholas Brealey Publishing, 1997.

Websites and blogs

Business networking

Rob Brown's blog www.therobbrown.com/connected-professional/

Joined Up Business Networking for Professionals www.joinedupnetworking.com

Keith Ferrazzi's blog on relationship building www.keithferrazzi.com

Andy Lopata's 'Connecting is not enough' blog www.lopata.co.uk/blog

Ivan Misner's 'Networking Now' blog http://businessnetworking.com

Dan Schawbel's 'Personal Branding' blog www.personalbrandingblog.com

Online networking

Joined Up Business Networking for Professionals www.joinedupnetworking.com

Just professionals www.justprofessionals.net

Social media

Chris Brogan's blog www.chrisbrogan.com

Mashable http://mashable.com

Cultural diversity

Cyborlink www.cyborlink.com

Executive Planet www.executiveplanet.com

Kwintessential www.kwintessential.co.uk/resources/country-profiles.html

Blogging software

Drupal www.drupal.org

Blogger www.blogger.com

WordPress http://wordpress.org and http://wordpress.com

Online community hosting

Facebook groups www.facebook.com/groups

Facebook business and community pages www.facebook.com/pages/create. php?

Downloadable worksheets and templates from Joined Up Business Networking – www.joinedupnetworking.com

- Client analysis worksheet
- Opportunity score brainstorm worksheet
- Online profile template
- Elevator/60-second pitch template
- Networking tools and processes worksheet
- Networking action plan

LinkedIn groups www.linkedin.com/directory/groups

Ning www.ning.com

Yahoo groups http://uk.groups.yahoo.com

Names and contact details of UK-based networking organisations

Referral generation groups

BNI www.bni.com

Business for Breakfast www.bforb.com

4Networking www.4networking.biz

NRG www.nrg-networks.com

Viva Business Networking www.viva-networking.co.uk

Mix-and-mingle events

The Federation of Small Businesses www.fsb.org.uk

Institute of Directors www.iod.com

Local Chambers of Commerce www.britishchambers.org.uk

Mastermind groups

Academy for Chief Executives www.chiefexecutive.com

Vistage's executive peer groups www.vistage.co.uk

Women-only networking groups

Athena http://theathenanetwork.com

Women in Business Network www.wibn.co.uk

WiRE (Women in Rural Enterprise) www.wireuk.org

Women's Unlimited Business Clubs www.womenunlimitedworldwide.com/business-clubs/

Parent-friendly networking groups

Mum's Business Club www.mumsbusinessclub.com

Mum's the Boss www.mumstheboss.co.uk

Social networking sites

Site	URL	Notes
Everywoman UK	www.everywoman.com	Female entrepreneurs, mainly UK based
Facebook	www.facebook.com	Largest social networking site in the world
Google+	www.google.com	Google's version of a social networking site
LinkedIn	www.linkedin.com	'Facebook for professionals'
Pinterest	www.pinterest.com	Social networking site based around the concept of sharing images
Plaxo	www.plaxo.com	Online address book

Site	URL	Notes
The small business community forums	www.smallbusinessforums.org	Community for small business owners
Startupnation	www.startupnation.com	Community of start-up business owners
SunZu	www.sunzu.com	Business owners from all over the world (previously called Ecademy)
Twitter	www.twitter.com	Micro-blogging site
UK Business Forums	www.ukbusinessforums.co.uk	Mainly UK SME business owners, but a good international presence
UK Business Labs	www.ukbusinesslabs.co.uk	Mainly UK-based SME business owners
Xing	www.xing.com	Similar to LinkedIn with a large European community

Index

How do you build your credibility, profile and reputation so that you are always in demand and in control of your career?

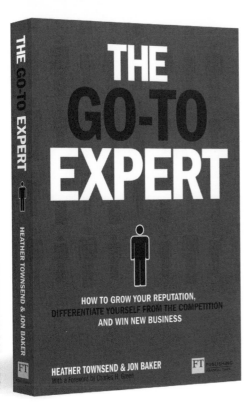

"If you want to move your career on, shifting from being just another professional advisor to being truly recognised as a go-to expert, this book will show you the way."

Richard Newton, award-winning author of *The Management Book*

"This easy-to-read book shows you how to build a firm foundation to win business regularly from your network. Highly recommended for any corporate professional or small business owner."

Charlie Lawson, National Director, BNI UK & Ireland

Available from all good bookshops

ISBN: 9781292014913

Enhanced with handy action points, chapter summaries and online worksheets, *The Go-To Expert* provides you with all the tools you need to grow your reputation *and* your business.

This no-nonsense guide will help you:

- Decide what you want to become known for
- Develop authentic ways of selling yourself
- Build your reputation through networking, writing and speaking
- Keep that phone ringing, as clients and opportunities seek *you* out

eBOOK
also available

FT PUBLISHING
FINANCIAL TIMES